METAVERSE INVESTING

CREATE, SELL, AND INVEST

William Richards

TABLE OF CONTENTS

INTRODUCTION

The metaverse is the next big bet between technology and social media. The idea of building a new virtual world as a direct evolution of the Internet is a greedy piece for many companies who are already thinking about the money (even virtual) that they will collect from users to sell them access to a new universe made of experiences. movies, concerts, meetings, games, and everything you can imagine in digital form. Think about your daily life and decline it into virtual format: meetings, lunches, sports, fitness, movies, trade shows, video games, and purchases will be converted to be available in the new 3D environment under construction.

It will take years (and billions of visors and smart glasses) to see the Metaverse in action at its peak power. However, some belief in it to the point of dedicating the name of the company to it, as did the former Facebook group, now Meta, which recently presented its hypothesis of an extended virtual world, explaining to users how it will be possible. invite friends, play, surf, meet colleagues or attend a concert without leaving your living room, in the blink of an eye. Meta is only the tip of the iceberg among companies in the world of technology and gaming: there are many examples of those who have invested heavily in the new virtual environment and who hope to reap the expected results during the next few years. That's why we decided to make this guide on the metaverse and what awaits us in the future.

What is the metaverse and where does the name come from?

Writer Neal Stephenson coined this word to describe the virtual environment in which the digital avatar of the protagonist of the novel Snow Crash, was released in 1992. metaverse through very often in its dystopian and alienating sense is mostly Ready Player One, where people spend most of their time in a golden virtual world in search of rewards.

You wear a headset or a pair of glasses and you find yourself immersed in a giant virtual city where you can decide what to do, just like you would click on a link in your browser. You can follow a meeting with office colleagues, go shopping as if you were in the supermarket, try on the new collection of your favorite clothing brands or play, draw, invite friends into your "digital" home, and so on. Within the metaverse, you can also buy virtual objects to show off with friends while you are online using Blockchain technology and NFTs to unlock exclusive content (such as works of art, sports tokens, or pieces of collectible films).

Which companies have bet on it?

We have already talked about Meta, but also Microsoft, Roblox, Epic Games, Tencent, Alibaba, and ByteDance have already invested millions of dollars in the development of the project. The Redmond-based company unveiled Mesh for Microsoft Teams which allows you to join video calls in an avatar version, providing a sense of shared presence in a meeting. The beauty of this idea is that you can do it from any device, without the need for special glasses or viewers, since Microsoft's cloud will take care of building virtual reality using artificial intelligence.

Roblox is setting up a real team dedicated to the development of games for the metaverse, while Epic Games - that is Fortnite - wants to see clearly how to implement it within its platform where, already now, you can attend concerts, films, and commemorations. virtual as in the case of Martin Luther King Jr. Alibaba wants to be ready for the explosion of virtual e-commerce, while ByteDance (which controls TikTok) is figuring out how to evolve videos in 3D format.

The problems of the metaverse

Net of the social dangers that come with retreating into a virtual environment, the metaverse will have to overcome certain hurdles to gain altitude. While the headsets, virtual reality, and platforms are already available or almost there are a few issues that inevitably need to be addressed. The first: who will manage the metaverse? The plausible solution is to rely on a non-profit organization that manages everything in the manner of what is currently happening with the Internet. And the second (closely linked to the first): will a single metaverse be enough or will we see dozens of them? It depends, if companies agree, building a single virtual world would be good for everyone: users, who could switch platforms like they switch sites now on the browser; and businesses, which may have a good user base to build on.

Once these two obstacles have been fixed, it will be necessary to think about the safety of users, the management of privacy, the influences on society from all points of view, and the technological hegemony that could be created. we still have a few years to find the right answers.

But there is no doubt that new businesses are also emerging, perhaps for everyone, even for users of the metaverse to earn, in this book we will show you what are the possible sources of income and how to make these investments.

CHAPTER 1: WHAT THE METAVERSE IS?

S ome time ago, Facebook announced that it will change the name of its parent company to Meta Platforms Inc. (Meta) during its annual Connect conference. This comes as no surprise to anyone who has been keeping an eye on the brand's latest hardware innovations.

In 2014 when Zuck acquired Oculus rift, we should have already understood something, the purpose of Meta is to go beyond software and integrate it into a hardware system that allows us to access the Metaverse. The democratization of VR viewers will allow us to bring the Metaverse into everyone's home. And while Instagram, Whatsapp, and Facebook applications will remain more or less like this, we will have a new Universe to discover thanks to virtual reality.

And the pandemic has enormously accelerated this process. And if the developers do a good job at Meta, this "Metaverse" could open the door to new work, social and playful possibilities that will impact your daily life. You just have to convince these 4 billion subscribers.

The Metaverse is best summed up as an online digital social space where people can meet, work and play collaboratively on a variety of devices. A key part of the experience is creating a digital avatar of yourself to help ground your presence in this next evolution of web interaction. Users can "enter" a virtual environment made up of interconnected worlds.

If you are inside the Metaverse using a VR headset such as Oculus Quest 2, you can communicate with others from a virtual environment of your choice represented by your digital avatars. Whether you're in a casual chat with a friend or a business meeting, you can talk to people in the real world via their phone or webcam, while they're displayed on a virtual screen in front of you.

When would Metaverse be released?

If we talk about the Metaverse developed by Meta "Horizon Worlds", the release should be official soon. But there are tons of other metaverses accessible. For example, The Sandbox, or the most famous Decentraland (which we will see today) without forgetting the pioneer Robolox. And all the virtual worlds that will be built by brands, government administrations, enthusiasts, etc.

What is Decentraland?

Founded in 2015 by Ari Meilich and Esteban Ordano and launched in 2017, Decentraland is a Metaverse powered by Ethereum and its native ERC-20 token known as MANA where users can purchase plots of "land" (virtual land), rent them, or monetize them. open virtual businesses.

Decentraland is also governed by a Decentralized Autonomous Organization (DAO) that allows token holders to vote on policies within the metaverse. The platform has grown by leaps and bounds and currently boasts a market capitalization of $6.8 billion (as of December 6, 2021). Non-Fungible Token (NFT) Sales Volume Reached $41.5 Million, this is Not Bad.

How do I access the Decentraland Metaverse?

The first time I tried accessing Decentraland Metaverse, I did it without a VR. You can easily access it from a computer, It's much easier to do than writing, but I'll try to be as specific as possible.

1. **Sign Up**
   There are two ways to access the Decentraland Metaverse, the first is through a wallet such as Metamask. When I opened my Opensea account to sell NFTs. The second is by logging in as a guest. Once you have gone to decentraland, just follow the instructions to register, so that in a few steps we can be inside the Metaverse with our avatar.
2. **Create your avatar**
3. There is no difference between it and a classic video game. I think the first time I happened to create an avatar was playing NBA 98 on Playstation 1. Nothing complex for anyone, you select the body, the face, the clothes, etc. Here different schools of thought, some prefer to have an avatar similar to reality and those who invent everything. This phenomenon of hyper-personalization was born in the days of Second Life, when already in the first years of the life of that Metaverse, you could buy skins or accessories to make your avatar unique.
4. **Familiarize with the environment**
   Decentraland, like other Metaverses, is virtual worlds dressed as videogames. Once inside, you will be guided by a tutorial that will give us the basic information to move our avatar. Press "c" if you want all the commands to appear on the monitor, move

with the keys "a", "w", "s", "d" etc. I believe that those who are already equipped with a viewer can experience more engaging navigation, also because moving in the virtual world, you can hear people talking, and in headphones, the stereo effect is a lot of fun.

5. **Interact And Navigate**
   Once the tutorial is over, the game is done, all that remains is to interact with the other citizens of Decentraland, navigate, wander around the neighborhoods and find out everything you can do!

Which metaverse should I choose? How to invest in the Metaverse? How to participate? So many plausible questions at this moment of incredible fervor. But my advice is always to test for yourself how this incredible new possibility works. I'm sure that in a short time, professional roles and careers within the Metaverse will emerge, so why not start being present in this primordial phase?

The Metaverse combines various elements of technology by uniting various worlds such as virtual reality and augmented reality where users can interact with each other within a digital universe. A universe where the blockchain will play a leading role.

Many imagine the metaverse as something unreal delegating it solely to the gaming industry. In reality, those who truly believe in the metaverse imagine real applications with users who can interact with their friends, work, play or take virtual trips around the world. A new way to live real experiences with the help of technology. We are still at the beginning of the development of the metaverse but there are already interesting applications. Not just video games, there are many other applications that we will see later.

The blockchain will be one of the technologies underlying the web3 and cryptocurrencies could be the gas of this revolution with for example utility tokens capable of creating a digital economy or the application of NFTs (non-fungible tokens) for the provision of services (ex: privileges, tickets for concerts or events, etc.).

Metaverse is a set of various elements of technology capable of uniting various worlds such as virtual reality, and augmented reality where users can interact with each other within a digital universe. We have therefore seen the definition of Metaverse and how this is connected to virtual reality applications.

So is the Metaverse just a different way of understanding virtual reality? Let's try to clarify the concept. The term metaverse is intended to represent a universe, a virtual world that can be explored by interacting with real elements, a sort of fusion with the real world. It's not just about putting on a pair of virtual reality glasses!

In this sense, we must also talk about the concept of augmented reality. For example, if you are using a virtual reality application it is possible to interact with the things that surround us but some things can be "added", that is three-dimensional objects that can complete our interaction. For example, if we are in a museum we could have a virtual guide that gives us insights when we get close to a painting. Or we are buying a PC and we can project on our table the PC we are about to buy in full size.

Other projects are also born for passenger car entertainment. The applications are endless and there are companies like Microsoft and Facebook (Meta) that are pushing on these technologies. Virtual reality will be a part of the Metaverse.

The technology behind the Metaverse is blockchain and NFT. This is a significant technological innovation that will therefore require the adoption of new technologies and the strengthening of current ones. A lot of companies are investing in the metaverse and this can certainly lead to the explosion of decentralized finance with the growth of the crypto sector but also of the NFTs that are still used today for the exchange of collectibles.

Today the most immediate applications are those of gaming and entertainment but we expect the development of an economy in which digital assets can be easily exchanged. A technological innovation fueled by decentralization that will surely lead to future regulation of metaverse applications.

Not sure where to start?

Before investing in the metaverse and on any asset, make sure you make the right assessments.

Companies that invest in the metaverse

Meta (Facebook)

Facebook believes so much in the Metaverse that it changed the company name to Meta. It is also towards that Facebook has been investing in this sector for some time.

Zuckerberg strongly believes in the development of Meta so much so that he thinks that Facebook will no longer exist as we know it. We are talking about the internet of the future, a platform where the virtual experience will be projected into the real world.

Microsoft (MSFT)

Microsoft had previously developed virtual reality applications with Microsoft Mesh. It also recently invested in gaming with the $ 69 billion acquisition of Activision Blizzard, Inc. (ATVI).

We are already starting to glimpse something with the operating systems leader who wants to bring avatars to his popular Microsoft Teams business platform as well. And let's not forget that after the Activision acquisition there will certainly be further development for video games and the growth of Xbox Live.

NVIDIA (NVDA)

Nvidia is one of the leaders in the processor and semiconductor industry. NVIDIA's chipsets are used now, not only in PCs but also on servers that perform complex calculations such as modern edge computing platforms.

We have seen that the metaverse can be defined as a digital environment that uses technology to allow users to interact with each other through augmented reality. Blockchain, NFT, and crypto will be heavily used in what promises to be web 3.0

The metaverse will allow the interaction of users in a digital universe in which, for example, users will be able to show the ownership of an asset, object, or asset through NFTs. In this way, authenticity will be guaranteed through the blockchain.

What are the main applications of the Metaverse?

We will likely see this technology applied to various industries such as work, entertainment, online shopping, gaming, digital art, finance, and real estate.

Since it is still just an idea, there is no single definition of the metaverse that everyone agrees on. What seems certain is that the metaverse could stand to virtual reality as current smartphones stand to the early, crude, cellphone models of the 1990s.

Unlike current virtual reality, which is mainly used for games, this new virtual world could be used for just about anything work, concerts, travel, and cinema. Or simply, as a substitute for leaving home to meet other people. How? With a 3D avatar, a digital representation of ourselves.

"We are at the beginning of a new chapter for the Internet, and it is also a new chapter for our company," said the founder and CEO of Facebook on October 28, 2021, announcing the metaverse and Meta, the new name of Facebook. A term that comes from the Greek word meaning "beyond". The first to talk about Metaverse was the writer Stephenson in 1992, in his science fiction novel The Snow Crash-.

In Stephenson's fantasy, the metaverse is imagined as an immense black sphere of 65,536 km in circumference, cut in two at the equator by a road that can also be traveled on a monorail, which has 256 stations, each 256 km away. In this sphere, each person can create in 3D what they want: shops, offices, public places, and more, all of which can be visited by other users.

It is a concept that somehow recalls that of the NFT (Non Fungible Token), linked to the blockchain, which in the last year have conquered the art world, with their certificates of possession of intangible assets. While making the necessary differences (bit techs like Facebook tend to be centralizers, while blockchain and cryptocurrencies are the work decentralized) both envision technological progress in more or less the same terms: something to escape reality.

Not everyone likes the metaverse

For example, Frances Haugen, the former Facebook product manager revealed in October that Facebook prioritizes profit over user safety and programs its algorithms to promote divisive content. Haugen is concerned about Meta's ability to control what is posted in the virtual world. In an interview with CBS, he stated that the same problems he denounced could be repeated in the virtual reality of the metaverse. "Facebook hasn't thought about security right from the design," he said.

According to Haugen, platforms like TikTok, where a small portion of the content generates the most views, are easier to moderate than Facebook's more distributed model. In virtual spaces where Meta is betting big, moderating content, removing misinformation, and tracking offenders will be a challenge because interactions are not logged.

A virtual reality, therefore. Something certainly not new. Its birth dates back to the 80s, by the computer scientist Jaron Lanier, with his company VPL Research, an acronym for Virtual Programming Languages. More than thirty years later, however, virtual (VR) and augmented (AR) reality of any kind have not established themselves as expected. Oculus VR, the virtual reality viewer created by the homonymous company acquired by Facebook in 2014, has remained nothing more than a gadget, at least at the consumer level. Virtual reality seemed to be the techno-utopian future. But, as Paul Skallas, the author of the Substack newsletter platform recently noted, "In 2000 you were told that virtual reality was about to explode, that it would change everything. It's 2020: where is it? ".

Virtual reality and AR at the same time have come across a big stumbling block: the habit of people relating physically. Instead of everyday life, therefore, VR and AR have established themselves more in the industry.

Which companies could be affected?

Again Facebook has experimented with a VR meeting app called Workplace and a social space called Horizons, both of which use avatar systems. Facebook's future workplace foreshadows virtual reality meetings where people use personal computers.

Another VR app, VRChat, is all about meeting online and chatting, with no goal or purpose other than exploring environments and meeting people. Other applications are just waiting to be discovered.

Similarly, when we shop online we will try on clothes in a digital, that is virtual reality, before ordering the ones that will arrive in the real world. It is now clear that we are witnessing the birth of "metaverse marketing", as defined by Forbes magazine.

Various realities of fashion and luxury are beginning to invest in virtual reality. Balenciaga sells "skins" on Fortnite, Gucci has put up a virtual bag only, Dolce & Gabbana obtained 5.7 million from the sale of 9 Non-Fungible Tokens,

Nike has decided to sell "virtual" shoes. According to Morgan Stanley, for the fashion and luxury sector, revenues deriving from virtual reality could amount, by 2030, to 50 billion dollars (about 44 billion euros). Normally, the multinationals in the sector are gearing up in this sense.

Applications in large scale distribution

Carrefour has purchased land equivalent to 36 hectares of land in the virtual world of the Sandbox video game. Created by the French studio Pixowl, Sandbox allows individuals and businesses to become owners of land and exploit it as they please. According to data from the OpenSea platform, the transaction cost the group 120 units of the Ethereum cryptocurrency, just under 300 thousand euros. Carrefour's director of digital transformation said that "events or product launches could be organized on this virtual territory.

Wallmart, the US giant of large retailers, filed on December 30, 2021, with the United States Patent and Trademark Office, several new brands that, according to the specialized media, would indicate its intention to produce and sell virtual goods, including electronics. , home decor, toys, sporting goods, and personal care products.

Metaverse and automotive

At the beginning of 2022 Hyundai Motor Company unveiled its new concept of Metamobility, a crasis between Metaverse and mobility. After announcing in September 2021 Hyundai Mobility Adventure, a metaverse space where users can experience Hyundai Motor's advanced products and mobility solutions of the future, the Group has decided to go deeper. It, therefore, decided to expand the role of mobility to virtual reality (VR), ultimately enabling people to overcome the physical limits of movement in time and space.

CHAPTER 2: HOW TO INVEST IN THE METAVERSE

———— ❀ ————

B y now everyone talks about it: the Metaverse is at the center of every discussion, as well as the main investment methods that concern it. Perhaps we are still far from a concrete concept of the "digital world", but for this reason, it might be the right time to understand its meaning well, study it in every detail and understand specifically how to make a profit.

In this guide we will try to direct everyone towards the best paths to take to invest in the Metaverse, focusing attention on its key elements and, above all, on the platforms further ahead from this point of view. We will address the issue of investment methods, but also the one that examines the "land" to be purchased, without neglecting even the risks that are run by following this new and unknown market strategy.

The Metaverse became popular soon after Mark Zuckerberg's statements. The CEO of Meta (formerly Facebook) has declared that he is working on a new completely digital world, within which anyone can be what they want and do what they want.

It can therefore be considered as a sort of evolution of the Web, currently navigable only through smart devices (smartphones, tablets, computers, smart TVs, and more). The Metaverse can also be visited "physically", thanks to some particular tools, and used to create a second life parallel to the real one.

Even here, there will be no lack of opportunities to buy properties, visit new places and meet other digital inhabitants. However, as also happens in the real world, everything will revolve around some source of wealth, even if at the moment it is not certain which type of "currency" will become the most popular. But let's go now into the main discourse of this guide, to understand specifically why we should immediately start investing in the Metaverse.

Risks and opportunities

As mentioned in the introduction, the Metaverse still turns out to be something quite immature and about which very little is known. The concept in the minds of tech giants is clear, but probably not so simple that it becomes a reality. However, the technology has never stopped and from year to year we have always managed to discover incredible innovations that were hardly believed possible. At this point, the question to ask might be "So is the Metaverse really that far away?"

Whatever the answer, one could still conclude that now is the right time to believe in this project and start investing to be able to have a "comfortable" life even in the digital counterpart of our life. Investing today means being able to follow the evolution of the Metaverse step by step, but also being able to buy and sell shares, NFTs, crypto, and so on at decidedly cheaper prices, compared to when the same digital world will seriously begin to take hold in everything. the world.

On the other hand, there is the risk of investing in the wrong currencies that may not be able to depopulate, or that this project may never really see the light. In short, like any other type of investment, even in this case it will be necessary to be very careful and hope to always be able to make the right decisions at the most appropriate time.

What we can do is, therefore, try to follow all those types of investments that seem most suitable for the Metaverse, discard the less probable ones, and focus attention on those that seem to have all the credentials to prove themselves adequate.

Actions

Let's start immediately with what for many represents the most standard concept of investment. Investing in the shares of large companies is certainly an optimal starting point, especially if you are aware of the companies most interested in entering the world of the Metaverse.

At the forefront, therefore, we can only consider Meta (formerly Facebook), probably the company that most of all were unbalanced in introducing the aforementioned project. It is easy to hypothesize that it also turns out to be the most advanced company in this sector and that first of all it will be able to make everything more concrete.

Microsoft should not be underestimated as well, which, with Windows Mixed Reality (formerly known as Windows Holographic), tries to compete with Meta for primacy. But the digital world is also about graphics, 3D, data analysis, artificial intelligence, why not, even video games. And what company is perhaps best placed to manage all this information if not Nvidia. In addition, the same company has also developed platforms dedicated to the development of the Metaverse, placing itself at the forefront of the race for the new Web.

ETF

When we talk about ETFs (or Roundhill Ball Metaverse) we refer to an investment concept that is certainly young, but which perhaps seems to be the most suitable in terms of Metaverse. The ETF is a sort of managed fund that acts passively and automatically analyzes the actions of the companies that seem to be most advanced in the development of cutting-edge technologies and the " Internet of things".

In the ETF we find the most famous companies, such as Microsoft, Nvidia, and Meta itself, but different realities could enter the sector at any time, such as Apple, Amazon, Roblox, Qualcomm, and others.

Cryptocurrencies for metaverse investing

Finally, this discussion won't be complete without mentioning cryptocurrency. Obviously, the Metaverse does not yet have an official currency and it is not certain that there will ever be one. However, it can be safely assumed that digital currencies will be the ones that can find the most space.

But we must not only focus on the most well-known, such as Bitcoin, Ethereum, and others, rather we must keep under control these seemingly smaller realities, which seem to point a lot towards the future and to be used in the Metaverse.

Among the many, MANA, the Decentraland gaming cryptocurrency, has managed to be touted as one of the most suitable, along with AXS, from Axie Infinity, and ENJ, a token already established for a few years, but which seems to still can't explode. absolutely.

The platforms where to invest in the Metaverse

Whether they are stocks, ETFs, or cryptocurrencies, you will always have to use the best and safest platforms for your investments. So let's try to understand which services it will be better to focus on.

EToro

Etoro is probably one of the most recommended trading platforms, as it sits at the top of the stock and cryptocurrency markets. In addition, thanks to its "social" sector, it will also be possible to learn from more experienced traders and learn how to buy and sell with greater awareness and ease. You need to know how CFDs work and if you can't afford to lose your money.

Plus500

Plu500 has always distinguished itself as a protected, flexible and open platform for different types of investments. Perhaps best for varying between investments focused on commodities, crypto, indices, forex, and various stocks.

IQ Option

IQ Option, on the other hand, focuses heavily on investment accessibility. Its service is available everywhere and therefore on any device, from the desktop to the laptop. In this way, it will therefore always be possible to keep all your movements under control, whether they concern stocks, crypto-currencies, or others.

Coinbase

If you are primarily interested in digital wallets and cryptocurrency, the advice is to focus on specific platforms, such as Coinbase. It turns out to be the easiest and most immediate platform to sell, buy and manage any type of crypto, from the well-known to the most emerging ones.

Coinsmart

A very valid alternative is given by Coinsmart, which is also mainly interested in the world of cryptocurrencies. It can indeed offer advanced tools to understand how to enter the world of online trading for the first time.

Coinhouse

Coinhouse instead presents itself as a very flexible service and able to adapt to any type of customer. Any private user will be able to open a free account in a short time, but there will also be more suitable profiles for different and more professional figures, such as companies and financial consultants.

XTB

For lovers of 360-degree trading, however, we cannot fail to also point out XTB, a leading company in the field of investments of all kinds: forex, indices, commodities, stocks, ETFs, and cryptocurrencies. All are available for commission-free sale and purchase up to a maximum of 100,000 per month.

Buying virtual land in the Metaverse

An important feature related to the Metaverse is that it examines the possession of virtual land. But what exactly are they and how can they be purchased? When it comes to investment, one cannot fail to consider the world of the real estate sector, among the most popular assets in the world. This concept can also be easily reported within the Metaverse since the latter will be divided into several digital "land", which can be purchased by users to be able to build properties and so on.

Buying digital land today means grabbing a large number of properties within the Metaverse. When the latter becomes popular, anyone will want to own a piece and in all likelihood, the prices will rise dramatically. In addition, by purchasing land, it will also be possible to create buildings, perhaps offering activities, managing overtime to generate a sort of easy-to-learn business. What is certain is that the real estate sector will once again have a particular value, even within a completely digital world.

Invest in the metaverse by purchasing virtual land

So how do you go about buying virtual land? Probably the best way to do this is through Decentraland, a platform that we have already introduced in the paragraph dedicated to the best cryptocurrencies to invest in.

Inside it will be possible to access a sort of marketplace, within which to use the Crypto MANA and LAND to select a plot of land, connect your digital wallet to the same marketplace, and finally confirm the purchase of the chosen property.

Final considerations

Before concluding, we would like to reiterate that investing in the Metaverse could represent an important risk, as well as an extremely fruitful source of income. However, we are convinced that proceeding today may be the best thing to do, to start immediately on the right foot and be able to improve your investments as the aforementioned digital world evolves.

CHAPTER 3: HOW TO BUY LAND IN THE METAVERSE

———— ❁ ————

B uying land in the Metaverse seems to be the hottest solution of the moment to invest in the innovative world of web 3.0 and Virtual Real Estate. Is it convenient? Let's see how to do it.

What do we mean by virtual earth?

Described for the first time in Snow Crash, a 1992 science fiction book, the Metaverse could be defined as a kind of deep virtual reality, shared in three dimensions via the internet, where it is possible to participate by being represented in all respects by an <avatar>.

Initially born as a completely futuristic project, last year it paradoxically experienced a real "materialization", thanks above all to a hype, where in reality everyone talks about it but few know it. Therefore, like any other new land to be repopulated, the first step is certainly about deciding which areas to subdivide and how to exploit them, through the distribution and sale of land, called land.

We could therefore define the lands as real virtual spaces, where inside it is possible to give life to social activities: open a playground, organize courses and events, or perhaps simply decide to rent it to someone else.

Currently, the best-known virtual platforms in the Metaverse where it is possible to buy land are two: The Sandbox and Decentreland. For the time being, both are making available a limited number of land areas, constantly monitoring changes in demand, to adapt the plots to their most easily marketable use and maintain their value within certain predetermined ranges. To date, the number of available lots on The Sandbox is around 90,000, while for Decentreland it is around just over 160,000.

What is virtual real estate and how does it work?

Before now, Metaverse users invested by buying land-only and exclusively through the use of virtual currencies, today a good part of the sales are also made in real money. And this has triggered and further reinforced among the developers of the Metaverse, also another concept, that of the management in open space of several plots of building surface.

Indeed, by buying more than one, it will be possible to access Real Estate, that is to say, a set of plots in the format 3×3, 6×6, 12×12, or 24×24. By managing more Estate of more players, they will even in the future turn into a real aggregate of lots, called a District (neighborhood).

The bet that many far-sighted real estate companies are making today is to try to think about how to be able to apply, to virtual worlds, the same rules studied for the traditional market, trying to envisage schemes and structures capable of promoting the sale in one way or another. of some elements, despite others. Proof which, in reality, has already been partially carried out by the creators of the Metaverse themselves. Indeed, deciding to buy a certain piece of land close to a famous figure in the entertainment world, rather than a great economist magnate in global finance, is already bearing fruit today.

Companies of Samsung, Intel, Tokens.com, and Nvidia caliber are investing heavily in the metaverse, assuming that the possibility of a favorable mid-to-long-term economic response may loom every day.

Buying land on the Metaverse is simple. All you have to do is register on your chosen gaming platform, log in with your avatar and immediately start browsing the land and all the items for sale in the appropriate catalog available for free, to check availability and prices.

Once factors such as neighborhood type, land size, and possible future developments have been taken into consideration, you can proceed to purchase via NFT cryptocurrencies, or the new virtual currency, by connecting a crypto-wallet (cryptocurrency wallets) and having the respective currencies (SAND for The Sandbox and MANA for Decentraland).

Why Invest in Virtual Land? (Advantages and Risks)

The last period has seen enormous growth in the economic-virtual world. Companies such as Microsoft, Facebook, and many others are investing ever greater quantities of resources and capital, to be the first to ride what appears to be the most relevant technological innovation of the next few years. Furthermore, cryptocurrencies are also developing more and more, see Ethereum, which favors the movements of this type of market.

Wanting to make virtual parallelism, if speaking of investment in the real world, brick is still considered the main element and with the greatest solidity over time, we could perhaps venture to think that the new structures that will be created in the digital world could to have some resonance even just for communicative osmosis.

We are still at the beginning, but if the advent of the Metaverse will take place in such a disruptive and massive way, as many seem to predict, then probably the investment could bring good results, provided that it is not just a whole big bubble.

CHAPTER 4: WHAT IS BLOCKCHAIN?

———— ❋ ————

B lockchain is a very recent invention, created by a person or group of people known as Satoshi Nakamoto, whose true identity is still unknown today. The blockchain can be considered as a digital register where many information (transactions) of different nature are recorded, this register is not physically located anywhere because it is shared between all the users of the network, for this reason, it is called decentralized and for the same reason cannot then be changed, allowing digital information to be sent but not a copy of it. Blockchain is a young technology but it is growing at a great speed. This is why it is one of the exponential technologies.

How does it work specifically?

The traditional way we used to share digital documents was to send a document to a recipient, who would be asked to make changes and revisions. The problem with this type of sharing is that to edit it again we had to wait for the other person to send it revised, otherwise we would have worked on two different files.

Today with online sharing systems available from different operators, both parties have access to the same document at the same time and the single version of the file is always visible to both. It is like a shared ledger and if someone decides to delete or modify important data, it is seen by everyone who is using the document at that moment. Obviously, we don't need the blockchain to use a shared sheet, but it helps us understand the meaning of a shared and decentralized ledger.

What does Bitcoin have to do with it?

The blockchain is made up of a network of so-called computer "nodes", a node is a computer connected to the blockchain network that uses a client that performs the task of validating and transmitting transactions. Each node receives a copy of the blockchain, which is automatically downloaded after joining the blockchain network so that the node is always up to date. Each node is an "administrator" of the blockchain and voluntarily participates in the creation and stabilization of the network, receiving in exchange the possibility of earning Bitcoin.

Each node competes with other nodes to earn Bitcoin by solving completely random math puzzles. Bitcoin was the very reason for the blockchain when it was first conceived in 2008, it is now recognized to be just the first of many potential applications for this technology.

There are about 2,000 Bitcoin-like cryptocurrencies (tradeable value tokens). Additionally, a number of other potential applications of the original blockchain concept are currently active or in development. Not just Bitcoin as well as other applications of the Blockchain too.

Currently, finance offers the most significant use cases for this technology, blockchain potentially eliminates the financial middleman like banks in almost any business. Personal computing became accessible to the general public with the invention of the Graphical User Interface (GUI), which took the form of a "desktop", likewise, the most common GUIs designed for blockchain are the so-called "wallet" apps, which people use to buy items with Bitcoin and store them with other cryptocurrencies.

Blockchain technology could, by solving some important issues such as scalability or confidentiality, replace intermediaries in any market, providing traceability and transparency.

CHAPTER 5: NFT

N FT stands for Non-Fungible Token is a type of cryptographic token that represents the deed of ownership and certificate of authenticity of a unique asset, both digital and physical, that cannot be replaced with anything else.

The good can be a drawing, a tweet, a gif, a video, anything digital can become NFT, defined as non-fungible because unique and non-replaceable but sellable in exchange for money.

Among the first NFTs were cryptokittens from the game Cryptokitties, but also the 5 thousand works of the artist Beeple, which sold for 69 million dollars, and Jack Dorsey's first tweet, which was sold for 2.9 million dollars.

How Do NFTs work?

NFTs are guaranteed authenticity and uniqueness because they are registered on the Ethereum blockchain, a cryptocurrency like bitcoin but which also supports these NFTs.

At the base of the success of NFTs is their uniqueness, these digital assets are designed to give you something that cannot be copied: the ownership of the work is exclusive to one person who owns the original, the artist who created it, however, retains copyright and reproduction rights, just as with the physical artwork.

In proof of the huge success of non-fungible tokens, auction house Christie's sold an NFT by digital artist Beeple for $69.3 million, which is $15 million more than Monet's painting, Water Lilies, was sold in 2014.

When are NFTs born?

The first NFTs come to the (virtual) world in 2017 as part of the CryptoKitties game that allowed the sale of virtual kittens, but the phenomenon exploded completely after a clip of LeBron James was sold, last January for 100,000 dollars.

Today there are videos of singer Grimes (Elon Musk's partner) sold for about $ 400,000 or gifs of flying cats for $ 580,000, as well as digital stickers, music, virtual plots of land and works by digital artists. To get an idea of what you can buy, take a look at the platforms dedicated to buying and selling such as Nifty Gateway, Rarible, or SuperRare.

Why Spend Millions On An NFT?

For buyers, Non-Fungible Tokens can represent intangible assets to sell or collect, while for sellers, digital creators, or brands, NFTs can become an important source of income. Furthermore, human beings love to be part of a community, also based on things they own, as is happening with NFTs.

An extremely popular community revolves around a collection of NFTs called Pudgy Penguins, but it's not the only one. One of the first NFT projects is the CryptoPunks, while now collectors and the Metaverse love Bored Ape Yacht Club.

What are cryptopunks?

Created by development studio Larva Labs, CryptoPunk is a series of 10,000 images tokenized as NFTs on the Ethereum blockchain.

The CryptoPunks are inspired by the English punk scene of the 70s and represent human and non-human faces with different characteristics, and the portraits of the characters were automatically generated by software that assembled the pixels. Today the least expensive Cryptopunk starts at $ 360,000 to alien CryptoPunk # 3100 which was sold for $ 7.58 million.

How are cryptopunks used?

NFT portraits are used as status symbols, showing them as a Twitter profile picture, for example, thus highlighting membership of an elite group.

Jay-Z, Serena Williams, Snoop Dogg, show off.

What is a bored Ape?

Bored Ape NFTs have now become a status symbol for the wealthy and digital investors. The avatars of the "bored monkeys", of which only 10,000 exist, have seen their price soar into the hundreds of thousands of dollars.

Each avatar of the Bored Apes is customized with different colors, designs, and accessories such as pink furs and sunglasses, which make them unique and inimitable. Owning a Bored Ape also means having exclusive access to a reserved club, the Bored Ape Yacht Club, where discussing your purchases, and participating in exclusive events and digital content, means being part of a close circle of privileged people. Among the owners of these precious NFTs are celebrities such as Jimmy Fallon, Snoop Dogg, Eminem, and Paris Hilton just to name a few.

How much does an NFT cost?

Today the least expensive image starts at $ 220,000 and the most valuable image is $2087, which sold for over $ 3.5 million. The total sales volume exceeded 1.8 billion.

The first bored Apes musical band is born

Universal Music Group, one of the largest music companies in the world, has announced the formation of a new supergroup called KINGSHIP, whose members are four Bored Ape Yacht Club NFT. The project was created by founder Celine Joshua in collaboration with Jimmy McNeils, a prominent NFT collector, who supplied the monkeys for the group.

In a statement, Universal Music Group said it "will lead the group in the development and release of new music based on the experiences in the metaverse and will usher in a new generation of artists, fans, and community involvement."

According to Joshua, each member of the group "has their own story and personality that influences and contributes to the overall narrative of KINGSHIP" - "Just like we would any artist or creator, my team and I will work with KINGSHIP to refine their vision and develop their unique sound ".

The group consists of a mutant monkey and three bored apes characters, including the rare Golden Fur monkeys and Bluebeam Apes.

NFT is the acronym for Non Fungible Token, which is a non-fungible asset. Let's take an example immediately to understand what it means. Let's say we have a book by our favorite author bought on Amazon. Well, that copy of the book is a fungible asset, because I and millions of other people can have it. But what happens if the author puts his signature on that book at some point? That book becomes unique because that very signature makes it unique among all printed copies. This is the principle of non-fungibility.

An example of fungibility is money. If I exchange a €50.00 note for another, the value remains unchanged. This is one way to explain the fungibility of something. Let's try to bring this discourse into the world of cryptocurrencies and blockchain. Take any cryptocurrency. If I have a bitcoin and you have a bitcoin, those two are fungible, because their value remains unchanged.

Non-Fungible Token: These are unique digital assets that cannot have copies. On a visual level, a digital asset can be replicated indefinitely, but it will always be a copied digital asset since the originality of a Non Fungible Token is given by the fact that it is printed and saved in the blockchain, which is a public ledger where all transactions taking place in the world in real-time are recorded.

Let's take an example:

- I paint a picture, scan it, and put it on the blockchain = I am the original creator and this is the unique content.
- I download the image of that painting, put it on the blockchain = I'm an impostor who tried to recreate an NFT using another person's content

NFT: Non-Fungible Token, unique non-editable digital objects

The types of NFT

Initially born as digital works of art, artists were the first promoters of NFTs. But beware, NFTs can go beyond the Art Universe and new ways are emerging every day to push and create non-fungible tokens.

For example, an application of NFTs can be linked to the world of gaming. Many software houses are sniffing the business to push and at the moment many games are coming out that can involve people also with the "earn to play" technique, which allows the user to earn money by playing.

Another application of NFTs can be linked to the Metaverse, with all the possibilities arising at this stage. For example, on Decentraland, virtual plots of land are for sale, where you can build, rent advertising space, open businesses, etc.

These are just some variations of NFT, but daily the categorization of these tokens is expanding dramatically including generative art, collecting, eCommerce, culture, music, etc.

We have seen that there are different types of NFTs, but not all of them have value. For example, if Beeple (a digital artist who became famous for selling his work for $ 69 million in the form of an NFT) releases new content, it will get a very different result than an NFT that I can make right now.

There are other areas:

Example 1: Gary Vee, a great source of inspiration for me and millions of other people, as well as an entrepreneur and visionary in the digital world, has launched a really interesting project, that is a collection of NFTs, which do not have much artistic value, but which have a value of content because whoever holds them has advantages or access to some services that are given by Gary Vee (discounts on courses, discounts on events, 1 to 1 sessions directly with him, dedicated communities, etc.).

Example 2: Flyfish restaurant, a real restaurant that will open in 2023 and which has bet on NFTs to offer customers a unique experience full of advantages, such as being able to access only if in possession of the token, guaranteeing a reserved seat, etc. Fun fact, one of the founders of this restaurant is Gary Vee

Example 3: Italian Wine Crypto Bank, the first Italian wine bank built on blockchain, based in Dubai and Hong Kong and with its virtual currency, the Iwb, to be used for the purchase of bottles. Many people think that NFT is just a trend, a bubble meant to burst or subside, but my sentiment, especially the numbers, doesn't seem to show the same situation. According to Bloomberg, the NFT market exceeded $40 billion in 2021. And to take a more concrete example, NFT trading on the OpenSea marketplace alone exceeded a few thousand sales and acquisitions in the last MINUTES!

I don't think the NFT phenomenon is a fad. The advantages linked to their development and their exchange are many, both for people and for brands ready to invest in this very promising and still not too well-known new market.

The NFT market is enjoying resounding success because so many people have managed to obtain unimaginable results. Riding this wave of successes, people's interest has increased tremendously and so NFT's stardom has increased dramatically. The art sector was the first booster to create interest around the thing and it seems that now we are in a phase of speculation and strong investment in the topics concerning crypto art, photography, art installations, 3d, etc.

ATTENTION, for people who earn millions many lose huge capital, so before launching headlong into the classic search for easy money, the advice given is to do all the necessary research. Also, I always specify that mines are only notes and not investment advice. Precisely because everyone should have a good understanding of how they can move and what they can do with NFTs. The ways to make money with NFTs are different and the approach can be taken from different angles when it comes to buying or selling Non-Fungible Token:

1. I can earn with NFTs by producing them
2. I can earn with NFTs by playing (play to earn)
3. I can earn with NFTs by buying and reselling them (flipping)
4. I can earn with NFTs by connecting services that I offer to those who hold them
5. I can earn with NFTs by buying Metaverse lands to rent or resell them
6. I can earn with NFTs by buying crypto art and then reselling

The first thing (I am speaking for my case) is to consider the risk. As fascinating as this world may be, one must always reflect on risk. What I invest is usually an amount that I am willing to lose if things don't go well.

Losing thousands of euros is much more frustrating and dangerous than losing a few tens of euros. So it is something extremely subjective and related to research. In technical terms, in crypto jargon, we say DYOR, "do your research". Before investing in artistic non-fungible tokens, for example, a good research procedure could be:

1. Understand what the project is about.
2. Inquire about the founders of a project.

3. Study well the "road map" which is usually shared on the official website of the project.
4. Check the social networks related to the project.
5. Verify the engagement of the contents that are shared.
6. Make sure the community is active and the founders are proactive.

It may seem complex to buy or sell an NFT due to the psychological barrier linked to the fact that the marketplaces are of a new conception (different from Amazon and the UX we are used to so to speak), there is a wallet to connect and the necessary money to buy cryptocurrency that can be used for economic exchanges. But in reality, it is not that difficult, once everything is set up, the purchase and sale of non-fungible tokens are immediate and user-friendly processes. As I always write, the best way to learn to understand how this Universe works is to try.

This is a new world, which has its roots in old practices that have been known for decades. The growth opportunities are so many and even for those who do not understand anything about crypto, investments, and trading, there can be room to learn, study and practice. As always, what I share on the blog is the result of my personal experience, so I do not sit in the chair to explain how it is done and how it works, but simply tell what I am trying to do, including errors, solutions, and problems.

CHAPTER 6: CRYPTOCURRENCIES

I n the field of new technologies, one cannot fail to mention cryptocurrencies. A cryptocurrency is a virtual currency based on the cryptography system, usable only by knowing a certain computer code defined by a public key and a private key, as in common cryptography. It is a (digital) bit representation of a monetary asset, devoid of contextualization in a physical factor (the minted coin)

Cryptocurrency is defined as a virtual currency, in the sense that it does not exist in physical form, but is exchanged exclusively electronically, whose transactions are carried out directly between two subjects in peer-to-peer mode, or directly between two devices, without the need for intermediaries (ie banks) to purchase goods and services, as if it were legal tender in all respects.

The cryptocurrency par excellence is Bitcoin, "forged" in 2009 and holder of over 50% of the world market cap. Cryptocurrencies are divided into "closed", "one-way" and "two-way" virtual currency. The difference between the three cases lies in the possibility or not of being able to exchange cryptocurrency with legal tender currency (such as bitcoins, for example).

Furthermore, one of the characteristics of crypto-currencies is the extreme volatility of their value, which often makes them very suitable for stock market speculation, rather than for use as a unit of account or means of payment, since it does would not be easy to establish the price of a product in Bitcoin for example, without linking it to the value of a currency having legal tender.

The Bitcoin architecture one of the very first examples of Blockchain is completely decentralized, offering a form of transparency and anonymity thanks to a distributed ledger-based on block transactions. Each time a Bitcoin is generated or used in a trade, it is validated and crystallized into a new block of the chain. This mechanism is based on a distributed logic, whereby in each block, within which normally no personal information flows, there is a hash of the previous block so that the manipulation of a specific block invalidates the entire chain.

How to manage cryptocurrencies (wallet and address)

Cryptocurrencies are stored in digital wallets (e-wallets, real virtual wallets), which can be both software (among the most common Jaxx.io which allows you to store numerous virtual currencies, including Bitcoin), hardware, or devices not permanently connected to the network, such as USB sticks, which are connected to the web via a computer, only when it is necessary to make a transaction.

The wallet is like a personal home banking service and allows you to store cryptocurrencies, transfer them to other users, receive payments, make payments, monitor the history of all transactions, and course to make purchases online, on sites that accept payment in virtual currencies. All in one software.

To work, a wallet must be connected to an address (or public key) which is essentially the equivalent of a bank account number. Normally, when a wallet is installed on the computer, this address is generated automatically and is represented by an alphanumeric string which, in the case of Bitcoins, is on average 33 characters, certainly not easy to remember. To receive bitcoins, it is enough to communicate this address to the interlocutor, and we will receive what has been agreed in a few minutes.

When the address is generated, a sort of password (or private key) is also generated which allows us to install this "account" on other wallets as well. In the case of Bitcoin, this password consists of 16 words, and it is good practice to keep it with great attention, perhaps by printing it and putting it in the safe, because in case of loss you risk saying goodbye to your (virtual) money since it does not exist. a password recovery service for addresses, since in the blockchain, there are no names and surnames, but only numbers and letters. The irreversible loss of the virtual currency contained in the wallet due to the loss of the access keys derives from the decentralization characteristics of the ledgers.

How cryptocurrencies work

Cryptocurrencies have peculiar characteristics that distinguish them. The constituent elements are shown below:

- A set of rules (called "protocol") that establishes the modalities by which participants can carry out transactions;
- A sort of "ledger" (distributed ledger or blockchain) that according to a block structure allows building a shared and immutable architecture on which the various transactions exist;

- A decentralized network of miners who update, store and consult the distributed ledger of transactions, according to the rules of the protocol and of the particular type of blockchain on which the virtual currency is built.

When we send (payment) via Bitcoin, we essentially send a candidate transaction to the blockchain, waiting to be validated by a distributed consensus system called mining that exploits a consensus algorithm (for Bitcoin it is Hashcash Proof of Work). To be "committed", the transactions must comply with the encryption rules established by the protocol and which will be verified by the network, otherwise, the transaction will be lost.

This operation is made safe by the blockchain paradigm technology, i.e. based on a ledger (a sort of ledger) that records all virtual currency transactions (including Bitcoin) in chronological/sequential order, according to a mechanism very similar to the digital signature.

The chronological recording avoids anomalous phenomena such as the so-called "double spending" (i.e. the attempt to spend bitcoins more than once at the same time), the concatenation of the blocks of transactions prevents the transactions carried out from being modified afterward, also because for to make a similar modification, it would be necessary to modify all the following transactions registered in the blockchain, which is, in fact, impossible also due to the high computing power required. The verifiability of the transaction takes advantage of the characteristics of chronology and sequencing, in this way any transaction can be traced correctly.

Finally, security is given by the fact that the blockchain is a distributed decentralized system, composed of nodes that record all transactions, and this distribution makes any attempt to modify the data impossible since the modification should be made on each node of the blockchain, and should be recursive.

Cryptocurrencies and smart contracts

Cryptocurrencies have cleared the concept of blockchain technology in other areas as well. The Ethereum cryptocurrency, for example, works differently from Bitcoin, although the mechanism is linked to the blockchain philosophy. Technically, Ethereum is a system that allows you to create smart contracts, the so-called smart contracts.

In general, smart contracts or "smart contracts" are software based on the blockchain paradigm, on a peer-to-peer system that distributes data between users on the network. These contracts work automatically and independently, without the need for intermediaries, verifying compliance with certain self-executing conditions and actions, or providing provisions so that certain actions can be carried out when the conditions are met and verified.

The benefits are many, including cost reduction, security against cyberattacks, and accuracy. The primary objective of smart contracts is to simplify procedures while protecting the parties involved, guaranteeing the integrity of data and information.

CHAPTER 7: WHAT ARE SMART CONTRACTS?

Smart contracts are simply programs stored on a blockchain that is executed when predetermined conditions are met. They are generally used to automate the execution of an agreement so that all participants can be immediately certain of the outcome without the intervention of intermediaries or loss of time. They can also automate a workflow, triggering the next action when conditions are met.

Smart contracts work by following simple conditional instructions ("if / when... then...") written in code in a blockchain. A computer network performs actions when predetermined conditions have been met and verified. These actions could include releasing funds to the appropriate parties, registering a vehicle, sending notifications, or issuing a ticket. The blockchain is then updated after the transaction is completed. This means that the transaction cannot be changed and that only the parties that have been granted permission can view the results.

A smart contract can contain all the necessary clauses to assure participants that the task will be completed satisfactorily. To establish the terms, participants must determine how transactions and their data are represented on the blockchain, agree on the hypothetical rules ("if / when ... then ...") that control such transactions, explore all possible exceptions and establish a dispute resolution framework.

The smart contract can therefore be programmed by a developer, although organizations using blockchain for business are increasingly providing templates, web interfaces, and other online tools to simplify the structuring of smart contracts.

Advantages of smart contracts

Speed, efficiency, and accuracy

When a condition is met, the contract is executed immediately. Since smart contracts are digital and automated, there are no paper documents to process nor waste of time dedicated to reconciling errors often resulting from manually filling in documents.

Reliability and transparency

Because no third parties are involved and since encrypted transaction records are shared between participants, there is no need to wonder if the information has been changed for personal benefit.

Safety

The transaction records of the blockchain are encrypted, which makes them very difficult to hack. Also, since each record is connected to previous and next records in a distributed ledger, hackers would have to modify the entire chain to change a single record.

Savings

Smart contracts remove the need for intermediaries to handle transactions and, by extension, the delays and costs associated with them.

Smart contract applications

Explore how companies benefit from smart contracts inactive blockchain solutions. Smart contracts on the blockchain to quickly resolve disputes with suppliers. With real-time communications and increased supply chain visibility, he is building stronger relationships with suppliers, allowing him to spend more time on critical work and innovation.

CHAPTER 8: WHAT IS ARTIFICIAL INTELLIGENCE?

Machine Learning, Robotics, and Neural Networks: so there are many areas for a single major technological challenge. Artificial Intelligence or Artificial Intelligence (AI) is a historically and scientifically very rich subject, which refers to an intimate human inspiration: that of creating a machine in which its capacities are fully reflected.

The history of Artificial Intelligence makes even more fascinating a paradigm that is already central in our process of progress and development. From the first intuitions of Alan Turing, passing through the strong/weak AI contrast of the 80s and the visionary scenarios of the beginning of the millennium (above all the film AI Artificial Intelligence by Spielberg), today Artificial Intelligence represents one of the main areas of interest of the computer science community.

The application areas are innumerable and many of these could have important impacts on the activities of companies and public administrations, as well as improve people's lives. And there is no lack of ethical and philosophical implications. In this guide, we are going to understand the role of Artificial Intelligence in the current context of digital and social transformation.

A definition of Artificial Intelligence

Although it is a complex technology, the underlying idea of Artificial Intelligence is very simple to develop machines with autonomous learning and adaptation capabilities that are inspired by human learning models. The concept of Artificial Intelligence moves from two distinct theories:

- **Strong Artificial Intelligence:** according to which machines can develop a consciousness of themselves, which studies systems capable of replicating human intelligence.
- **Weak Artificial Intelligence:** which believes it is possible to develop machines capable of solving specific problems without being aware of the activities carried out. The aim of this theory is therefore not to create machines equipped with human intelligence, but to have systems capable of performing one or more complex human functions.

Definition in hand, Artificial Intelligence is the branch of computer science that studies the development of Hardware and Software systems equipped with specific skills typical of the human being (interaction with the environment, learning, adaptation, reasoning, and planning), capable of autonomously pursue a defined purpose, making decisions that until then were usually entrusted to people.

In other words, Artificial Intelligence is a research field that studies the programming and design of systems aimed at providing machines with one or more characteristics considered typically human. Properties range from learning to visual or space-time perception.

In this scenario, Artificial Intelligence must be treated by combining theoretical aspects with practical and operational ones. Starting from the meaning of AI, in this guide, we can describe the main Artificial Intelligence techniques (Machine Learning and Deep Learning above all), the functioning, the different applications, the resulting opportunities Answering a final thundering question: Artificial Intelligence is a threat or a necessity for man?

The applications of Artificial Intelligence

At the base of Artificial Intelligence, there are algorithms, computational techniques, and solutions, therefore able to replicate human behavior. All these applications of Artificial Intelligence can be multiple and concern different fields, not only industrial but also domestic. Think, for example, of home automation systems capable of regulating temperature, humidity, or lighting based on our habits or the use of our voice as input for some devices, which facilitate the management of our homes and, in general, our standard of living. A remote control (even a smartphone) or our voice is enough to activate Artificial Intelligence systems that facilitate the management of our homes.

However, if it is true that Artificial Intelligence could be applied to different areas of our daily life, this diffusion process is not destined to spread to all areas at the same speed. To provide a complete picture of the Artificial Intelligence solutions adopted (or adaptable) by companies, we identify six classes of solutions, distinguished according to the purpose of use.

CHATBOT

Among the various Artificial Intelligence applications on the market, the Chatbot is one of the most popular solutions among companies, here we are talking about a tool capable of offering 24/7 assistance to both its customers and employees, which also lends itself to various uses in marketing, sales support, HR Management, home automation and even Research and Development.

NLP (NATURAL LANGUAGE PROCESSING)

NLP techniques aim to create systems capable of promoting human/machine interaction and understanding. NLP mainly deals with texts, that is any sequence of words that in a language express one or more messages (such as web pages, posts, tweets, company information).

COMPUTER VISION

Computer Vision studies algorithms and techniques to enable computers to achieve a high-level understanding of image or video content. Advances in recent years have been such that solutions based on statistical descriptions of images have progressively given way to neural networks trained on millions of images.

IDP (INTELLIGENT DATA PROCESSING)

The class of Intelligent Data Processing solutions is the broadest from the point of view of applications. This includes all those solutions that use Artificial Intelligence algorithms on structured and non-structured data for purposes related to the extraction of the information present in the data. The main purposes that move companies in using these solutions are Forecasting Classification & Clustering.

RECOMMENDATION SYSTEM

Recommendation algorithms are today the main pillar of the business model of all social and eCommerce platforms (Amazon, Netflix, Spotify, but not only). At the base of many digital services, some algorithms keep track of the user's actions and, by comparing them with those of others, they learn his preferences and are increasingly able, as the user uses the platform, to produce more precise recommendations.

PHYSICAL SOLUTIONS

It is a guided means of transport, autonomous Robots (robots capable of moving without human intervention), and Intelligent Objects (objects capable of performing actions without human intervention and making decisions based on the conditions of the surrounding environment).

There are many theories and applications related to artificial intelligence, and in this scenario, understanding in depth how AI works is not easy. This man versus machine is a timeless dispute. There are still many ethical and legal issues related to artificial intelligence. There are as many doubts about what the impact of Artificial Intelligence will be on our society and the world of work: we wonder if this technology is a threat or an opportunity if machines will replace humans if artificial systems will be more capable and more intelligent than human beings.

CHAPTER 9: VIRTUAL REALITY

———— ❄ ————

O ur body and therefore our senses are used from birth to interact with everything around us. With the birth of electronics first and then of information technology we also began to talk about how to create "parallel worlds" and around the mid-1950s specific studies began on how to stimulate the senses through simulations; these simulations of environments were carried out using multisensory stimuli and the studies produced a project that resulted in the construction of a sophisticated, for the time, a machine called Sensorama.

The first example of digital reality as we know it today was created in the late 1960s with the studies carried out by Ivan Sutherland at the University of Utah and which allowed the construction of the first virtual reality viewer.

What is Virtual Reality? What are the developments and environments in which VR (Virtual Reality) already gives and will be able to make a significant development contribution in the future? To answer the first question, it must be premised that basically, Virtual Reality is an exclusively digital environment created by one or more computers that simulate actual reality and recreates it in an intangible way and that is conveyed to our senses using consoles that allow interaction. in real-time with everything that is produced within that world; this data exchange is allowed by computer devices, mostly vision goggles, touch gloves, and earphones for hearing, and allows complete immersion in the simulation created in a three-dimensional and dynamic way by accessing a whole pre-ordered series of contents that are explored to build a real and true parallel world.

As already mentioned, in the early sixties there was the first realistic approach to a digital reality; Sensorama can be defined as the first and so far only complete Virtual Reality device as it was able to stimulate all 5 senses (with stroboscopic images for sight, loudspeakers for hearing, aromas and smells for smell and taste, air flows through the face and neck and a handlebar for the hands and arms for the touch; it was also equipped with an armchair equipped with counterweights and levers for the sensations of the swaying of the body and balance; currently it is giving instead a considerable importance to sight also in consideration of the fact that this is considered the dominant sense, which is why all virtual environments are developed with very high visual qualities, therefore capable of proposing themselves as effective substitutes for reality. It must also be considered that Virtual Reality is divided into immersive and non-immersive:

Immersive Virtual Reality, in the first case the user is completely isolated from the external environment and is transported into the parallel reality reproduced and is completely absorbed in it thanks also to a complex set of accessories that integrate professional viewers such as the Oculus Rift;

in the second case, on the other hand, the digitally recreated environment has a lower emotional impact on the subject inside the goggle and this also happens due to the quality of the viewers: in the Samsung Gear VR, for example, it is the smartphone that serves as a which recreates the virtual environment, which is inserted in a special housing inside the viewer.

The architecture of Virtual Reality

The architecture necessary to be able to take full advantage of Virtual Reality is composed of viewers that have certain characteristics such as a field of view from 100 to 110 degrees, a frame rate (frequency of images projected per second) between a minimum of at least 60fps and a maximum of 120fps to avoid a jerky vision annoying to the eyes, a gyroscope that allows, together with an accelerometer and a magnetometer, the so-called Head Tracking or the displacement of the image following exactly the movements of the head along with the four points cardinals and with response times from fifty milliseconds to thirty milliseconds.

All this is deliberately developed to ensure that the user can interact and "live" within virtual reality and in the real world when we hear a noise, we turn our gaze towards the source of the sound; this in Virtual Reality is allowed both by the presence inside the viewer of a professional multi-channel audio system that offers the sensation of sounds coming from all directions and that allow the so-called Doppler effect (with the increase of the approaching sound and the decrease in the distance) and by a sophisticated infrared pointing system that allows you to read the eye movement (the so-called eye-tracking) making immersion in the virtual environment even more realistic by creating depth of field.

Virtual Reality VS Augmented Reality

Virtual Reality VS Augmented Reality In many cases Virtual Reality is confused with Augmented Reality; in fact, the latter is enrichment and strengthening of the perception of the real world through a series of digital contents and additional inputs that allow you to have a deeper knowledge of the environment that surrounds us of a specific part of it and above all, not being immersive like Virtual Reality, it does not necessarily need specific viewers but can be easily observed on everyday devices such as smartphones or special screens (as in the case of car accessories). Virtual Reality is, therefore, together with the Cloud (of which it can exploit the infrastructure), Artificial Intelligence (of which it exploits the Machine Learning mechanisms), and Big Data (of which it exploits the amount of data and filters algorithms and research), the new frontier of software development; a very famous example of collaboration between these infrastructures was Nintendo's interactive Pokemon Augmented Reality game which exploited the scalability of the Cloud and Big Data profiling algorithms to give hunters the ability to view Pokemon in real-time.

Applications of Virtual Reality (medicine, architecture, and fashion)

To better explain this concept of adaptability, let's make 3 examples of the application of Virtual Reality in three very distant fields: medicine, architecture, and fashion.

Medical field: Virtual Reality is becoming not only an educational tool but also a therapeutic and operational one, with the most famous epilogue in April of a year ago at the Royal London Hospital where the first surgical operation took place in connection with India of the story in VR broadcast in real-time; in the field of both physical and cognitive rehabilitation, Virtual Reality can simulate daily steps with increasing levels of complexity allows you to perform a sort of personalized training of the patient within a safe and controlled system accompanying him from the onset of the pathology (such as an accident or illness) up to a gradual reintegration into society.

In the surgical field, Virtual Reality (and especially Augmented Reality) allow for operation in very difficult and highly dangerous situations such as those between the brain and the torso; taking advantage of the third dimension there is the possibility of observing details not visible to the naked eye thanks to an exocamera operated by the surgeon and through the images that are amplified on a monitor, it can act with greater precision by limiting the area of the intervention and increasing both the effectiveness of the operation is a faster recovery of the patient. In the medical field, Virtual Reality also allows for a very in-depth range of tools for an even earlier diagnosis of neurodegenerative diseases such as those suffering from Alzheimer's or Parkinsons through a neurosensory reactivation based on memories of real events experienced in the past.

Another aspect of the fundamental importance of Virtual Reality in medicine is in the field of education, training, and updating; the ability of VR to be able to faithfully recreate environments allows students to simulate interventions and operations of any type or diagnosis without having to intervene directly on the patient but in an equally realistic way; to give an example, an osteopath can easily act on the virtual patient's spine without risking making him paraplegic, or a surgical specialist can, in the first few times, carry out an entire operation, from anesthetization to stitching and much more in Virtual Reality.

Virtual reality and building design: is another field in which virtual reality has become dominant in the design of buildings, both for construction, renovation, and interiors, with a clear distinction and integration between the design in 2D, CAD, and VR; in the first case you watch how the result of the idea should be through design software while with virtual reality you experience the result; we avoid these unpleasant feelings of difference between the original idea and the real result such as the positioning of the furniture requested by the client or the installation of a certain type of lighting. Thanks to immersive 3D rendering software, it is also possible to build and explore virtual buildings and houses before construction begins, so that you can check for any design flaws and avoid costly modifications.

The last example concerns the field of fashion where instead virtual reality allows you to wear clothes with the accessories related to them before buying them and without having that annoying (for some) need to go and try them inside a dressing room by scrolling. all the warehouse of the store, and without having the anguish of finding the right size. Augmented Reality finds a lot of space in fashion, above all due to its lower need for infrastructure power: instead of viewers, there are goggles equipped with cameras that allow, for example, to see a certain model of dress in multiple shapes and colors simply by looking at the model that is positioned in front.

Fashion: it could be the arm of a futuristic project combining Virtual Reality and Artificial Intelligence, or the possibility of entering a virtual world that is always in constant evolution and that modifies, for example, its own space depending on what we wear (if we are in a suit the environment is a beach if we are in a jacket the proposed environment will be a mountain).

The union between Artificial Intelligence and Virtual Reality on Cloud Computing platforms is therefore already something very close to the realization of what until a few years ago was only the fruit of a sci-fi cinematic imagination. Do you need to worry? Each new technology has its dark sides and, especially at the beginning of its history, has detractors who imagine catastrophic changes, but innovation and research are an integral part of human nature. It is how the various discoveries are used that make them useful, harmful, or dangerous; in the case of Virtual Reality, the greatest danger (especially if associated with Artificial Intelligence) could be that of a gradual detachment from everyday reality in favor of a world that always follows our desires but at the same time allows us to have unthinkable tools that allow a significant gain in quality of life.

CHAPTER 10: AUGMENTED REALITY

---※---

What is augmented reality and how does it differ from virtual reality? As a premise to this topic, it seems only right to give a general definition of "augmented reality", and then specify in the next paragraphs the different details of which it is composed. In this context, I have long searched for a specific definition on the subject and the one that seemed most convincing among the many is the following. I found it on Whatsl.com:

Augmented reality represents an integration of reality achieved through the use of technology. A series of digital information (animations and new content) is added to the surrounding environment using a device (smartphone, PC, special glasses, etc).

I know that right now you will be speechless, hoping to understand the concept behind this tangle of words. For this, we will now give an example, so that everything is clearer. Try thinking back to a few years ago when Pokémon Go became popular. Surely you have already heard of this application or even downloaded it to your smartphone or seen it used by your children and/or grandchildren. Maybe you've even found a Pokémon on your bed with special attention! Seriously, this application has perhaps become the quintessential example of augmented reality: in practice, once downloaded, the application used the camera and the Internet connection to allow the user to come across Pokémon more varied. The goal was to catch as many Pokémon as possible in every country and city in the world.

These creatures could be found in a street, on a glacier, even in a fountain short anywhere.

Pokémon Go became a worldwide phenomenon within weeks of its release, with 21 million users in the United States alone using the app daily in the summer of 2016 to track down Pokémon in the region. where they resided (and not only!). If these numbers seem like hot air to you and you think it's pointless to have millions of users if you don't get money in your pocket, keep this other data in mind: they are on the day of release of the game, the estimated amount for Pokémon Go was equal to 4, 5 million dollars. At the end of 2016, the app reached almost a thousand million dollars.

Over time, of course, the phenomenon has faded, but what this app has brought to the whole world was the awareness of the importance reached by augmented reality. This technology is, in fact, able to add digital details to the surrounding environment (in this case, your city) to enrich it with elements not perceptible to the five most common senses (Pokémon). All this happens through devices, common (PC or smartphone, for example) or specific (lenses and glasses).

Ah, but then we are talking about the much better known 'virtual reality! Maybe that's your exclamation right now. Be aware that this is not the case, virtual reality and augmented reality represent two distinct concepts and it is good to know the differences so as not to fall into the error of confusing them. The main difference between these two types of technological realities is the level of immersion.

Virtual reality allows you to create a new, "ideal" environment with fictional characters. It is therefore a 100% simulation of reality. An example of this is The Sims, the well-known game in which you create an alter-ego (a "Sim", in fact) and build him a house, a family, and friends. In short, there is a total simulation of real life, which however takes place in a virtual environment, with virtual characters. In practice, virtual reality completely replaces the real with the artificial.

As already mentioned, however, augmented reality refers in all respects to the real environment to add details, whether they are Pokémon, cars, or furnishing items. That is, it takes its cue from the reality that surrounds us to show digital elements. As you may have guessed, in essence, both virtual and augmented reality make use of technological devices, but in different ways, as you have seen.

Based on the examples set out so far, would it be correct to say that augmented reality is used purely to create video games? And, above all, if so, what would it have to do with the business and why should it be useful for an activity, or rather, your business? By definition, when it comes to "augmented reality", the head flies to the world of gaming. Let's say that this particular digital method finds its best application in video games, both on smartphones and PCs. But not only. As we will see later, augmented reality can also become a valid tool for a company: many multinationals have already noticed this and have begun to exploit this tool for different purposes. These companies have realized that improving the potential customer experience through an app that uses this method can represent a significant added value to create an interaction with the potential customer and increase sales.

CHAPTER 11: OMINIVERSE AVATAR OF NVDIA

—※—

At the GTC 2021 web conference, Nvidia announced Omniverse Avatar, a technology platform for generating interactive avatars based on artificial intelligence. Omniverse Avatar combines Nvidia technologies in the fields of artificial intelligence, computer vision, natural language comprehension, suggestion engines, and simulation technologies. The avatars created on the platform are interactive characters with fast-tracking 3D graphics that can see, talk, chat and understand the purpose of natural speech.

Omniverse Avatar-Nvidia pointed out that this opens the door to the creation of artificial intelligence assistants that can be easily adapted to any industry. For example, these assistants can help businesses manage countless day-to-day customer service activities, restaurant orders, banking, appointments and reservations, and more.

Omniverse Avatar is part of Nvidia Omniverse, a virtual worlds simulation and collaboration platform for 3D workflows currently in open beta with over 70,000 users. And that's not the only Omniverse-related news unveiled at the GTC conference.

Nvidia Omniverse Replicator is a powerful synthetic data generation engine that produces physically simulated data for training deep neural networks. The artificial intelligence company has introduced two applications for generating synthetic data. One for Nvidia DRIVE Sim, a virtual world designed to host autonomous vehicle digital twins, and another for Nvidia Isaac Sim, a virtual world for robot digital twins for manipulation tasks.

These two Replicators allow developers to launch artificial intelligence models, bridge gaps in real-world data, and label field information in ways humans can't. The data generated in these virtual worlds can cover a wide range of different scenarios, including rare or dangerous conditions that cannot be experienced regularly or safely in the real world. Autonomous vehicles and robots built using this data can also master the skills in a variety of virtual environments before applying them in the physical world.

CHAPTER 12: THE DISNEY METAVERSE

D isney also looks at the metaverse, the fusion of the physical and digital worlds that allows people to communicate virtually. This seems to be the future of the big web giants, but not only Disney shows. According to the current CEO, Bob Chapek: "The initiatives we have carried out to date are merely a prologue to the moment when we will be able to connect even more closely to the physical and digital world, making possible storytelling without borders to the inside our Disney Metaverse ".

The project described so far points to a technological leap in virtual reality for California's international entertainment company. "My vision is to use Disney + as a metaverse platform," Capek said in an interview with CNBC fast money. "The project aims to use digital and physical components on a 'three-dimensional canvas' that narrators can draw on to create experiences typically found only in amusement parks, movies, or books: all of which can be combined without limitations, boundaries, or limitations. Our creators are already waiting for the metaverse to speak about the technical equipment needed to live these stories, Chapek clarified that "the viewer" may be present, but not everyone has to use it, the helmet may not be in our plan. "

The issue of digital devices, as an access point, was mentioned by Tilak Mandadi, in a post on LinkedIn as early as 2020. The former vice president of digital described the possibility of creating a sort of theme park in the metaverse, as an innovation in the Covid context to live unique but social experiences shared with other users thanks to augmented reality, artificial intelligence, IoT, and the help of wearable devices, smartphones or other.

At the business level, the horizons that could be opened are many, almost a century after the first cartoon with synchronized sound, Steamboat Willie (1928). "We aspire to create unparalleled opportunities for consumers who want to experience everything Disney has to offer, from products to platforms, wherever they are," Chapek added. "As we look to this next frontier, and given the unique combination of our brands, franchises, physical, digital experiences, and global reach, we see the limitless potential that excites us more than ever as we look forward to the next centennial of the Walt Disney Company." will be celebrated in 2023.

In the past, Disney has already made forays into the digital world, for example, the children's social network, Club Penguin, closed in 2017 after eleven years. In the field of social gaming, it bought Playdom for $ 563.2 million in 2010, and in 2014 it acquired Maker Studios, a multichannel network with a strong presence on YouTube, for $ 500 million. In 2016 he launched Disney Movies Vr, which provides an immersive experience of select Marvel, Lucasfilm, and Pixar movies using the Oculus headset.

CHAPTER 13: SNAPCHAT

S napchat? Ah yes, I think I heard about it a few years ago. But why, does it still exist? Well yes, despite the common thought that imagines this social network is now in oblivion, the Snapchat app is still very popular and downloaded in all parts of the world. Moreover, many international companies and brands continue to exploit the features of the platform to increase their reputation, build an online presence and find potential customers.

In short, Snapchat is still a valuable social network. As Wearesocial's Digital 2021 report shows, it is still among the most used social networks around the world with 498 million active users. Well, let's start with the basics. We can define Snapchat as a service halfway between a social network and a messaging app. In fact, in the now distant 2011, its creators Evan Spiegel, Reggie Brown, and Bobby Murphy launched it in the market precisely to allow users to be able to send private messages.

Three characteristics distinguished this social network from the others that already exist:

1. The ability to send audio and video messages of up to 10 seconds (the so-called snaps) that self-canceling after viewing.

2. The presence of the stories, videos, or photos published by the user in real-time but which lasted only 24 hours before disappearing forever.
3. The use of filters.

Do these three elements remind you of anything? Is it a coincidence that the evolution of Instagram took place precisely by integrating these new features?

Snapchat had become one of the most loved and downloaded applications by teenagers all over the world, precisely because of its innovative aspect. Instagram then began to feel the weight of the competition, to the point that Mark Zuckenberg even attempted to buy it and acquire it in his application arena, but got a resounding "No, thanks".

By then he had only one option left which was to copy. This is how, in a short time, we saw stories, chats, and filters appear in our Instagram home. In short, without Snapchat, we would not have Instagram as we live it today.

How Snapchat works

Well, let's get to the point. How does the platform in question work? The interface is very intuitive, so once you have downloaded the app and created the account it will be very easy to learn how to use it. But we want to make this step even faster for you. Let's start with the basics.

How to create an account

Go to Google or Apple Store and download the Snapchat app. At this point you need to create your account; personal information will therefore be requested.

Click Register and enter the requested information: name and surname, date of birth, email address, password, username, and mobile number. Right on this device, you will receive an SMS with a confirmation code that will allow you to securely verify your account. At this point, it is time to explore.

The main features of Snapchat

Simplicity, immediacy, and creativity are the keywords of this social network. Here are the main things you need to know to get started with the platform:

CAMERA: On the main screen you will immediately have access to the camera with which you can start taking pictures, create small snaps or make stories;

CHAT: It is essential to communicate with other users, and exchange messages, photos, and videos.

CREATIVE ELEMENTS: Filters, stickers, geofilters, free designs, and much more to make your snap unique;

NOTIFICATIONS: By clicking on the bottom right you can access notifications and stay up to date on everything that is happening.

Well, now that you have met the protagonists of this social network, it is time to analyze them in detail to understand how to use the platform.

1. Create a snap in a few steps

As we said, as soon as you open the app, access to the camera will immediately appear with which you can create your content before publishing it. In reality, the true value of a snap or a story lies in the special effects; there are all kinds, and it's up to you to choose how to give free rein to creativity.

Among the main Snapchat effects for editing images and videos are:

- **Filters** i.e. drawings to be superimposed on photos or videos. You find them at the bottom of the screen; swipe right and choose the one you like best to create fun and creative content;
- **Lenses** are 3D graphic effects to add to your face.
- **Geofilters** graphic elements to be inserted based on the geographical place where you are.
- **Free drawings** and **personalized texts** are inserted by tapping anywhere on the screen you can add personalized captions or draw with a digital pencil

After creating the photo or video, you can decide how long the user can view it, whether to save it in the personal gallery or whether to add it only to the Stories (they only last 24 hours, remember). Finally, once the story has been created, it will also be possible to:

- Decide who will see the content (everyone, just friends or a small circle of specific contacts).
- See who viewed it.
- Delete the story before 24 h.

2. Snapchat chat (how to exploit it)

We began by saying that Snapchat started primarily as a messaging service (the word chat in the name is no coincidence). Therefore, it allows its users to send messages in all possible formats.

How do you do it?

- Just click on the cartoon symbol in the app, then search for the contact and start the chat. At this point, you will be free to write text messages, send photos, audio, snaps, stickers, etc.

- Not enough for you? With Snapchat chat, you can also start phone calls or video calls just like with Whatsapp or Messenger.

3. **How to view a snap**

Once we have seen how a snap is created and how it is shared through stories or chats, we also want to introduce you to the viewing mode. If someone sends you a snap, you will be notified. From there, click and you will be redirected to the message area; at this point enter the chat with the friend who sent you the message and view the content. As we said, this will disappear soon after. To keep it you could make a screenshot but, be aware, that the other user would know.

4. **See Snapchat notifications**

Like any self-respecting social network, Snapchat also has an area with notifications. Here you will find:

- Updates on stories and snaps posted by your friends.
- Discover, is a section where you can see stories posted by brands, famous people, or influencers.
- Live, an area where snaps related to specific themes or events appear.
- My Story is a catalog with the snaps you published in 24h and a summary of who viewed and screenshots them.

5. **Follow and add friends**

Once you know how it works, you can start working on your profile by adding friends and acquaintances. Just click on the icon with the ghost symbol, click on "Add friends" and choose the way you prefer to find your contacts. In detail you can:

- Type the name of the contact you are looking for.
- Use the snapcode (i.e. a scannable code such as a QR code).
- Take advantage of the feature to add close friends.
- Synchronize the phone book and import all contacts to search for them in the social network.

How to delete a Snapchat account

Snapchat app

OK, all clear. Let's imagine instead that we have the opposite situation; you have already owned your account for a long time and are tired of using Snapchat: how do you cancel? You can delete your account at any time. Just enter the app, swipe up, and click on the Settings icon. In the search bar, type "delete account" and you will be offered the corresponding solution. Select it, enter the password and confirm the cancellation. The game is done. For the first 30 days, the account will only be deactivated, afterwards, it will be permanently deleted!

Snapchat for business (tips to take advantage of social media and be successful)

Snapchat is not dead, indeed it still seems to be one of the most used social networks by Generation Z. Therefore, if you have a company and your target is between 16 and 20 years old (or a little more) you cannot rule out the possibility to create a company profile on Snapchat.

Here are some tips to take advantage of the platform's full potential and be successful.

- Post frequently (remember that the contents disappear after 24 hours), but don't overdo it! 3 to 4 posts a day will do just fine.
- Storytelling is the secret. Telling a story is always an effective solution to interact with the public, attract attention and generate interest.
- Be interesting. Snapchat is not a frivolous social network, made up only of filters and stickers; relevant content is always favorites. Therefore, create meaningful campaigns that add value to users' lives.
- Create custom filters and lenses. Snapchat offers an ad hoc service to help brands customize their special effects.
- Create custom coupons, and offer discounts and promo codes.

Pros, cons, and risks of Snapchat

Using creativity is, therefore, Snapchat's greatest strength. The value of this social network lies, in fact, in the ability to edit photos and videos with special effects, and use filters to create fun content and geofilters to personalize them. Furthermore, another great advantage consists in the self-destruction of the contents: in this way you do not run any risk that someone can go and recover your old photos.

However, there is always the option to take a screenshot, which makes your privacy much less controllable. In addition, Snapchat appears to have no secure encryption systems like other messaging apps and, above all, does not place limits on the types of content to be published.

For these reasons, this platform is often used by teenagers for the practice of sexting. That is, aware of the fact that the messages are deleted after a few seconds, they feel free to be daring and send personal and sexy photos. Unfortunately, the risk is around the corner: just take a screenshot and spin the photo between your contacts to transform a private moment into a destructive situation, which can lead to cyberbullying and revenge porn.

This advice is therefore always the same for all social networks: pay attention to the contacts you add, divide the intimate sphere from the public one and use social networks to have fun, learn and socialize!

In conclusion

Here we are, at the end of our journey to discover Snapchat. Now it should be clear to you what this social network is, how it is used and how it can be exploited to be successful with your business.

The lens was presented called Avatar and is applied in augmented reality on the face, transforming it in real-time into that of a video game character. The new filter is also a suggestive and potential response to a need that is becoming more and more urgent, namely the graphic representation of oneself in the metaverse. Paradoxically, however, Snapchat's new AR lens could breakthrough not so much on the app for which it was designed as on TikTok, as has happened recently with other lenses.

The operation of Snapchat's new augmented reality lens is very simple, you choose from the list of AR filters and frame your face. From that moment, you can take pictures or even shoot videos and the algorithms will manage the information in real-time, following the movements of the face without ever dropping the virtual mask. The lens is free and available to all users who have downloaded the app on Android or iPhone. The final effect smoothes the skin by making it uniform and accentuates the colors and lines of the lips, teeth, eyes, and eyebrows.

The semblances created by Snapchat's Avatar filter could be very close to the proposals being prepared by giants such as Meta or Microsoft and even Disney, which are already engaging a lot in the increasingly thriving metaverse market. In fact, in addition to clothing, the creation of one's avatar in virtual reality is becoming an increasingly important requirement, but also a delicate one since it has to deal with the toxicity generated by unrealistic representations (not only external) typical of modern social networks.

CHAPTER 14: MATTERPORT

———— ❋ ————

Born to capture real places in 3D and make them practicable virtually, Matterport technology aims to break down the barriers between the physical and digital world. It integrates with Autodesk Bim 360. A tool that allows you to digitally recreate spaces in 3D and that initially had a strong development in the real estate sector, wherein practice it offered the possibility to real estate agencies to show houses, villas, and apartments remotely, highlighting every single detail and allowing customers to virtually visit a property just as if they were walking through it.

Matterport 3D, produced by the California company of the same name, is a camera that can reconstruct the interior and exterior of buildings in three simple steps. Thanks to the combination of 360 ° panoramic photos, the system surprisingly reproduces real spaces and environments both indoors and outdoors with a strong emotional impact.

In short, an effective tool for those working in the real estate sector, where a real explosion took place during the pandemic months, as expected.

In reality, however, this technology has much broader fields of application, precisely because it is capable of transforming real-life spaces into immersive digital twin models and of returning interactive and virtually viable virtual places.

This tool has all the characteristics to work also in the tourist-cultural sector (for online visits to exhibitions, museums, and sites, monuments), in the sector of large-scale distribution, and of course, in the field of architecture, engineering, and plant engineering. where it offers the advantage of increasing the accuracy and speed of construction, reducing construction costs.

Matterport is based on an application that can accurately and quickly document any type of property: it offers the possibility of capturing all the spaces with a high level of detail and exporting the collected data to other platforms. The system provides a series of transversal services with the creation of digital twins that allow you to manage all phases of the project up to implementation, promotion, and maintenance.

It offers all those who collaborate the possibility to virtually connect and work together from different places and also to perform remote inspections and measurements.

The program has several applications for creating navigable virtual visits as well as streamlining space exploration, not only for business purposes such as the real estate sector but also for constructive and organizational purposes. The scans are, in fact, photographic reliefs in every sense, highlighting all the dimensions and volumetric aspects of the building through point clouds.

The platform can also extract high-resolution photos equivalent to 134 megapixels. Digital twin measurements are more than 99% accurate and virtual tours can be accessed from anywhere, from any device.

The functionality of Matterport Notes helps increase collaboration between all parties involved and makes the integrated project planning workflow more efficient. The program allows you to start conversations between team members, and add mentions and hashtags, as well as direct links, attachments, and notes. This makes it easier for users to track progress and receive notifications when files are open or when someone has commented.

Exploring virtual spaces also has several advantages in terms of logistics. For example, internal 3D mapping can be used to share three-dimensional panoramic views of the structure with employees, as in the case of a new workplace so that they can familiarize themselves with the premises and their organization before physically going to the site. : A kind of online orientation to get a priori information about building properties.

Surrounding virtual reality also becomes a useful tool for training employees operating in complex contexts, inaccessible or potentially dangerous areas. This is because Matterport also generates complete schematic floor plans where emergency routes and response strategies can be planned.

How to use Matterport?

It starts when you turn on the 3D camera. You can choose either the PRO2 3D model, which guarantees 99% dimensional accuracy, or the Leica model, which achieves up to 99.9%. Both have a battery with eight hours of autonomy. The camera must then be connected to a mobile device (tablet or smartphone) via Wi-Fi via Matterport Capture which you download from Google Play.

After positioning the tripod, you can continue scanning. Each lasts 20 seconds, which is the time it takes to scan a room 360 degrees. The distance between one scan and the other must not exceed three meters, as the correct overlap of the images is essential for the correct acquisition of all details.

However, the application provides step-by-step feedback on the quality of the scans and their alignment. In practice, this technology automatically queues scans and uploads to the cloud to generate a 3D model in seconds. The cloud offers a perspective in dollhouse mode with a top view of the rooms to see the building as a whole, the scaling and layout, the surrounding visit, and the point cloud.

CHAPTER 15: THE SANDBOX

———◦❋◦———

C an you make a video game based on a metaverse that combines voxel-style graphics, a fully open game editor, NFTs, blockchains, and cryptocurrencies? The answer is yes and it has a specific name: Sandbox! Sandbox is much more than a video game, but it is a platform that goes far beyond gaming. Are you ready to enter the era of the metaverse?

The sandbox is a community-led metaverse, or rather a web platform that reproduces a structure similar to the real world: some users inhabit it, the territories to buy, the places to visit, and the objects to use. The peculiarity is that this virtual world is connected to the Ethereum blockchain, and any digital element including characters is treated as an NFT (Non-Fungible Token) that can be created, purchased, and exchanged.

All elements of Sandbox such as avatars, objects, buildings, vehicles, and the experience on the platform can be created directly by the community using two main tools: the three-dimensional graphics editor VoxEdit and the Game Maker software. The potential is therefore virtually endless, as it is the users themselves who can develop the desired game or interactive experience.

The currency inside the platform is called SAND and is, of course, a cryptocurrency that allows you to make any type of transaction inside and outside the Sandbox. To access the sandbox, you need the digital wallet to which your account is linked. The world in the sandbox is made up of virtual plots of land called LAND with only 166,464 LAND, a fixed number that will not be increased in the future. Each LAND can communicate with others through specific portals.

Everything is for sale

The important thing to understand is that everything is for sale on The Sandbox. Using SANDs, inside the metaverse you can buy the NFT of the art services you see in virtual museums, you can sell your products with VoxEdit to other users, you can get a landscape for it to build an interactive experience. on it, placing a ticket at the door.

To purchase NFTs and experiences within Sandbox go to the integration store or OpenSea site, where LANDs are also sold. The trades are made by SAND, but obviously, everything is also linked to the real world, as the SAND can be converted to Euros, Dollars, or other currencies.

Everything can be monetized in some way, even the experiences themselves, you can become a tour guide, bring in new users for a walk for some advice, or you can learn the best fighting techniques for homes a strict prison offers sports with a few ballets and even. made some impact on some dedicated EARTH. As mentioned, the power is so great, that only the imagination of the user is read.

What can be done at the moment?

Sandbox is currently at the Alpha level, so we are still at the beginning of your adventure. However, what we have done so far is a lot, the developers have provided all the tools to create elements and experiences, we have selected LAND, some existing maps, and games, but above all has become residents with users.

Alpha Level is a small museum building and some areas with different biomes. Then there is the NFT School, which has a lot of art in it by some well-known artists, and the Snoop Dogg studio. You can visit Dum-Yz's Dungeon, a one-player experience in which our enemies, weapons, and platform elements: a small game to test the combat system and game skills, all good for an experimental title ruler.

XYZ Garden is a kind of cultural venue where you can have many experiences, including events, celebrations, and interactive moments. The club is open from today 2nd December, so maybe one of the first to take a tour inside.

The impression is that of being in a world halfway between Minecraft and Second Life, in which you have enormous room for creativity and you can put on complex experiences, based on living and constantly moving communities.

Graphically, maps are a triumph of colors. The voxel-style elements are always very nice to look at, but in the museum objects of exquisite workmanship have been produced, with a very high level of detail. The only concern concerns the performance, which at the moment is not ideal: we are still in an Alpha, as mentioned, so there is plenty of time to fix this aspect too.

The future of gaming (beyond)

We repeat that the capabilities of The Sandbox are truly endless. Not just for the game team, but everything else. As for Second Life, Minecraft, and Fortnite, this type of platform allows you to host events and social moments rather than the video game itself.

The final version of the Sandbox is expected to arrive in 2022. But it seems that the first interest in the altar is too high. Some big companies and people - such as ADIDAS, Atari, deadmau5, Snoop Dogg, The Walking Dead, and others have already jumped on the bandwagon and created their virtual worlds. There are many more coming in the coming months, so there is a lot of meat on fire for those who want to have fun on The Sandbox.

If you also want to try the Alpha version of Sandbox for free, just go, sign up and start playing immediately. For those who want the perfect experience, there is also the option to purchase Alpha Pass, which entitles you to 1,000 SANDs, 3 NFTs, and some exclusive content. Below we leave you with some pictures of the metaverse, including current and world views.

CHAPTER 16: METAHERO

---※---

Metahero was recently launched the Binance Smart Chain (BSC) project that combines 3D scanning technology with non-exchangeable token smart contracts (NFTs) to enable the creation of unique meta-avatars objects and meta-objects. At the heart of Metahero is 3D scanning technology that analyzes a real-world object to gather data about its appearance and make it digital. To access the best 3D scanners, Metahero has partnered with Wolf Studio, whose technology has been used in the music, gaming, and fashion industries.

Metahero provides its users with the ability to turn almost anything into a highly realistic NFT. But simply recreating something digitally is only part of the value. Each Metahero NFT is registered unchanged in the blockchain and is instantly monetizable. Metahero builds a market and a symbolic ecosystem to provide entrepreneurs and creators with access to a unique and fully digital future. Metahero's story begins with the start-up Codewis in Krakow.

Codewise was acquired in 2020 and its CEO, Robert Gryn, took $ 10 million in the proceeds and committed it to self-finance its vision for the metaverse. Although Metahero was formed in 2021, Gryn is deeply involved in web 3, in particular, as an angel investor in Tenset, a bridge between the traditional stock market and cryptocurrencies. Metahero's team includes numerous Codewise alumni and a rapidly expanding cast of developers, engineers, and community builders.

How does metahero work?

MetaHero scan

Metahero scanners are a technological innovation. Each uses a mobile 3D camera consisting of 16 mobile posts with a server unit and four cameras. In addition, there are a total of 64 devices ready to capture images in perfect sync.

To provide users with access to 3D scanning, Metahero plans to build scanning chambers in strategic locations around the world. To begin with, it is planned to install 12 rooms in areas with a strong technical and game culture. Their first generation 4K public camera is already operating in Doha, Qatar. The next cities are Tokyo, Berlin, New York, Seoul, and many more.

All it takes to use Metahero scanning is to download their app and keep a certain number of HERO tokens, the platform's native asset, in your wallet to pay for the scan. Metahero charges around $200 for a full-body scan, which is relatively below average.

Metahero APP

The Metahero app is another pillar of the Metahero ecosystem. The first iteration of the app will serve as a vehicle for holding and trading HERO tokens. Subsequently, the app will also allow users to license NFTs, track all metrics related to their HERO activity, and function as a launchpad.

Integrating the app with the Fiat system is a vital part of Metahero's strategy to drive mass adoption. Currently, to get

HERO and participate in next-generation 3D scanning, users need to acquire BNB tokens on BNB Smart Chain and then purchase HERO via PancakeSwap, a process with some friction.

Once subsequent versions of the app are completed, users will be able to skip this friction and switch from their local currency to HERO in just a few clicks. Metahero also has aspirations to integrate with Visa, which would allow HERO holders to spend tokens on day-to-day expenses.

Token HERO

The HERO token is a utility token that allows a user to access the Metahero ecosystem. The token uses a new deflationary model that reduces total supply over time. HERO offers its owner the ability to transact on the Metahero NFT market, pay royalties or finance their scans.

The public sale of HERO took place in June 2021 via the Tenset Gems platform. The launch and public presale were followed by an IDO on Pancakeswap in July 2021. The total supply of the HERO is limited to 10 billion and blocking mechanisms are in place to discourage token dumping. Given its focus on mass adoption, Metahero demands an environment with convenient and fast transactions. And according to the team, the HERO token was launched on BSC with scalability and inclusivity in mind.

What makes metahero unique?

There are countless crypto projects focusing on NFT and gaming, but few add 3D scanning to the mix. Metahero is therefore an answer to the question, what would it be like to inject yourself on the internet?

By building a bridge between the physical and the digital, the Metahero team is contributing to the fact that the future is not less about flying cars, but about finding synergies between emerging technologies. Using AR, VR, cloud server, blockchain, and ultra-HD scanning, Metahero aims to create something completely new.

If the project is successful, Metahero will be a critical link between digital and physical. And it will become a major player in the early colonization of virtual worlds with unlimited potential for self-expression and value creation.

CHAPTER 17: AXIE INFINITY

A xie Infinity is one of the most popular games in the world. Game battles in Axie Infinity have become an advantage for many players, as they can be earned by playing. Axie Infinity is a game based on virtual animal husbandry, based on a chain of blocks, and offers players the opportunity to fight in two modes: arena or adventure.

Players can breed, collect, trade, and fight through acquired creatures. With good strategies, a player can make a profit through a method and implementation that allows him to exchange them for physical money. Launched in the blockchain of Ethereum in 2018, Axie Infinity is a Pokemon-inspired Role-Playing Game (RPG) where players can fight, collect and raise pet-like creatures called "Axies".

While Axie Infinity was a success for the game alone, the game's interaction with blockchain technology was truly groundbreaking. The team at Sky Mavis, the company behind Axie Infinity, used the blockchain to develop an affordable design in which players are rewarded for the game.

With a vision that work and play can become one, the game has won a lot of fans around the world. The long-term goal of the platform was to introduce blockchain technology to a larger percentage of the population. It was a huge success, like many early players set aside large sums of money through prizes.

According to Axie Infinity documents, the game currently earns more than 13,000 ETH (over 14 million euros) in revenue and is currently the number one computer game based on Ethereum. In fact, within the game, it will be possible to win real cash prizes (in cryptocurrencies), which can then be used to move forward in the game, buy NFTs, or enter the world of online investments using the currency created by Trung Nguyen himself. It is certainly not the only online game that offers such possibilities, but we can consider Axie Infinity as one of the main ones in the current world panorama.

As mentioned above, Axie Infinity can almost be considered a tool to allow everyone to know the world of cryptocurrencies, offering, instead of the usual fictional coins, real Tokens that can be used in real life.

How to make money with Axie Infinity gaming?

It will be enough to buy, breed and have animals (called Axies) fight against other online users all over the world. The more challenges you win, the greater your chances of earning. You have to buy a starter kit, which will already include 3 Axies at the basic level. However, if a friend, family member, or acquaintance is already registered in the game, it will be possible to be invited and avoid purchasing the basic package, as it will be provided with the invitation.

The tokens that can be used during the game will be essentially two: SLP and AXS. Both will be earned by winning challenges, passing levels, and completing missions and can then also be used to buy items, improve the characteristics of their Axies, or take them out of the game to start a real adventure in the world of investments.

SLP

The SLP, or Small Love Potion, is the official currency of the game. This will be obtained in all phases of the gameplay and can be used to go on in the adventure, buy useful items in the game store, evolve the priori animals, or even be exchanged in US dollars.

AXS

AXS, also known as Axie Infinity Share, is the currency underlying the entire project, which can then be used, buy, and sell on online trading platforms, and which gave life to the game.

To start playing Axie Infinity, you'll need Ronin's cryptocurrency bag, as the game runs on the side chain of the same name, not Ethereum. At the same time, you must have a MetaMask to transfer RONIN to your wallet. The transferred cryptocoins are used to purchase 3 creatures on the patent market, which is a necessary condition for gaming.

Creatures named Axies depend on their characteristics (they currently cost $ 36). There are nine classes (reptile, plant, sunset, sunrise, aquatic animal, bird, beast, insect, mechanic) that differ in six characteristics (mouth, eyes, back, tail, forehead, eyes). Each Axie has a score based on four attributes called "statistics": health, speed, skills, and morale (details here). Buying creatures is a crucial moment, as choosing the right ones can make the game easier (more chances are more expensive). The game has two arena and adventure modes. Adventure mode is for learning to play, fight, or perform everyday tasks. Arena mode (PVP) is where the battles between players take place. In practice, the two teams compete with each other using the cards at their disposal: each creature has four that correspond to its four characteristics and thus to its abilities. In each turn, the player chooses which card to play to maximize his chances of defeating his opponent.

SPL which stands for Small Love Potion, is the ERC-720 token that the player receives when completing tasks and winning battles. It is used to reproduce the Axies and to participate in events and competitions (in these cases the tokens are "burned" or removed from circulation). This type of token is available in an unlimited number of copies, so its value tends to drop (to overcome this problem, the rewards of SLP in adventure mode have recently been removed and the "burn" mechanisms increased).

The SLP value is also related to the number of plays in the game. The more of them, the greater the value, and vice versa. I have players from the Philippines, Venezuela, and Brazil who use it as their main source of income. But how much and how can you earn with Axie Infinity?

The average daily gain depends on the fluctuations of the cryptocurrencies but is around 50 dollars. Players can earn income by winning tournaments, selling Axies and land, or breeding their creatures. The latter method allows you to generate rare monsters that can reach huge figures (in October one was sold for 250,000 dollars). However, it must be considered that there are limitations and costs. Since Axie Infinity is a game that requires a large investment, another way to play has been created, scholarships allow you to get started on the platform without that investment.

Getting a scholarship is a simple method, among which you will find some methods that are suitable for obtaining it:

- Search through social networks for someone who provides this scholarship service on the platform. Look for tips and guides before filling out the form. On the official Axie Infinity Discord there is a dedicated section for applying for scholarships.
- Get a scholarship through a friend or acquaintance who has Axies attacked and who may not need it, especially if you already know the person, the trust will be earned.
- Take into consideration the scholarships that the platform itself offers through its system. Start forming your team in Axie Infinity with scholarships without having to invest first.
- Keep in mind that trust is important and that searching the networks or pages can have both positive and negative consequences, one of which is that you run out of profits. Always be careful.

How much money could you earn if you opened your account?

Income is an important detail if you decide to invest and not opt for a scholarship. Opening your account can be profitable, in adventure mode it's around 75 SLP per day, and depending on the conversion, it can be around $ 360 or more.

Although it is less than the investment made on the page, it is a large amount that can rise and fluctuate if the price of SLP can fluctuate. Making opening an account an important decision, especially if you can sell purchased axles at any time.

How to download Axie Infinity on your device?

The process to download Axie Infinity is very simple, what is fundamental is a stable internet connection, after which you only have to carry out the following steps:

Download and create an Ethereum wallet. Find Ronin Bag and make one. Remember to set it up and keep all the keys. Go to Axie Marketplace and log in using your Ronin wallet. Activate your account, and set up your email and passwords.

After these steps, all you have to do is enter the Axie Infinity page and click on the "Download" area, located at the top right, select the platform or device, and voila, you will download and you can start playing.

CHAPTER 18: DECENTRALAND

---※---

Decentraland is a project born in 2015, which came to maturity only a few years ago when it was officially made available to the public. In short, it is a virtual world in which people or companies can buy spaces and objects to develop the most diverse experiences. So that's what we'd call a metaverse today, and a few years ago we would have defined "something like Second Life" or even Habbo if you were a kid in the '90s. Since then, many things have changed, both in terms of computing power and network infrastructure, and, most importantly, blockchain technologies have developed.

The spaces within Decentraland can represent everything the developers decide to create: museums, shops, places to chat with other people, stand for product presentation (Samsung itself has unveiled the latest smartphones there), and gaming experiences. all kinds of games, from first-person shooters to driving games, to Minecraft or World of Warcraft clones. The suffix -craft, which in English can mean art or craft (but also the act of creating or putting together something), is the very soul of the project.

How Decentraland works

The world of Decentraland is divided into plots, 16 square meter plots of land that anyone can buy and combine with adjacent land to create a space big enough to accomplish what they have in mind. In addition, for some of these spaces, there is a specific graphic or theme that places them in a specific neighborhood, much like what happens in amusement parks, or as has happened many years ago. years within Geocities, where all the sites that talked about cinema were contained in the same directory. The first example of this organization is Genesis Plaza, a virtual plaza located in the center of the map where you can learn more about all of Decentraland, how to use it, and what the hottest neighborhoods are.

Each Parcel is associated with an NFT on the Ethereum blockchain, so it is unique, not replicable, and cannot be confused with the others. Inside are the coordinates that place the plots of virtual land on the map and all the information necessary to visualize it in space.

The paradigm shift of Decentraland and similar projects, according to its creators, is that unlike other virtual spaces owned by a single entity, there cannot be full control over content by a central entity that censors and bans. Everything would be managed by a Dao, a Decentralized Autonomous Organization, which would allow collective management of Decentraland and guarantee that all participants could vote for any extension or improvement. The problem is that the ability to vote is directly related to the amount invested. The Dao also controls the most important smart contracts, i.e. blockchain information related to leases, objects within Decentraland, etc.

A world regulated by virtual currency

The virtual currency to shop within Decentraland is called Mana, which began circulating in 2018 after an initial sale offering raised $26 million in about 30 seconds. At the moment each Mana is worth around 2.80 euros and the price of a Parcel can vary from 1000 or more, it depends on the real estate market and where it is located. Once you have purchased a virtual land, you can decide to decorate it using the internal editor, create custom virtual objects or buy those created by others.

In recent months, there has been more and more talk about the Decentraland (MANA) token, under the magnifying glass of crypto enthusiasts due to some particularly interesting aspects concerning it, first of all, its possible key role within the metaverse.

Unsurprisingly, Decentraland's price has risen significantly since Facebook founder Mark Zuckerberg officially announced his new company name Meta and the start of work on implementing virtual reality.

The digital currency MANA is seen by analysts as one of the altcoins with the most rosy long-term growth, which is why it is recommended to purchase and store some quantities in your digital wallet. Fortunately, crypto is available on numerous exchanges and the procedures for purchasing it are relatively simple.

As anticipated, Decentraland (union of the English terms "decentralized" and "land") is the name of an open-source videogame platform built on the Ethereum blockchain. The creators of the virtual space are the Argentine developers Ari Meilich and Esteban Ordano.

After creating their avatar, users who participate in the gaming experience can buy and resell many lots of land to build on. The currency used for transactions is MANA, Decentraland's native ERC-20 token which, unlike other cryptocurrencies, cannot be mined and is removed from the blockchain each time a transaction takes place for the purchase of land or other assets that can be purchased. by users. In addition to buying or selling land, MANAs are used as currency to buy digital content, NFTs, advertising services, and more. The crypto is listed on numerous exchanges and in recent weeks its price has risen by more than 400%, an aspect that has sparked the interest of analysts and beyond. Several investors expect the uptrend to continue in the coming years and cross $15 by 2025.

How to buy MANA tokens you need to follow a few simple steps:

Find an exchange they are listed on: Decentraland's crypto is available on over 30 exchanges. Given the wide choice, it can be difficult to find a reliable, safe, and usable reality.

Create an account: the registration procedure may change depending on the platform chosen, but in general, it will be necessary to provide your name and surname, email address, and mobile number. The creation of an account does not take long and is usually completed in a few minutes, at a later time the platform will also request the sending of documents to verify the user's identity (identity card, bank statement, residence, etc.) in compliance with anti-money laundering legislation.

Depositing funds: to start buying MANA or other cryptocurrencies you need to send funds to your account. The main exchanges provide for the possibility of depositing money by credit or debit card, bank transfer, or directly in cryptocurrency, in case you already have Bitcoin or other currencies.

Buying MANA: proceeding with the actual purchase is a simple operation and it is sufficient to follow the instructions on the website of the exchange that you have chosen to use. If you do not want to proceed with the purchase immediately but prefer to wait for Decentraland's prices to drop, you can set purchase orders at the desired price. It is good to monitor price fluctuations and analyze forecasts daily.

The Decentraland platform is a DAO (an acronym for "Decentralized Autonomous Organization"), i.e a project that is not managed and regulated by a central entity but by the indications present in its smart contract. In other words, the developers do not own the game environments and cannot modify them to their liking. To take part in the governance of Decentraland it is sufficient to have the following tokens:

MANA: they are the version blocked in the Decentraland Blockchain of MANA and are obtained through the exchange of the latter.

LAND: they are the non-fungible tokens that represent the lots of lands that each user owns. Each LAND has its characteristics and cannot be replaced by another.

While each MANA has a single vote, only one LAND grants 2,000 votes, so owners of many LANDs can exert more weight on future decisions. Most of the time, LANDs are grouped into districts, which are very large areas created by players who share a common passion, such as music or the visual arts. The lots of land for sale can be viewed in the appropriate marketplace, which indicates the value in MANA and any buildings present on them.

CHAPTER 19: FACEBOOK HORIZON

The beta version of Facebook's Horizon Workrooms is a new virtual reality experience that allows you to work together, having the feeling of being in the same room even if very far apart. So the tech company wants to revolutionize remote working.

Facebook's Horizon Workrooms, through a post published by Mark Zuckerberg, was presented as a new virtual reality collaboration platform. The platform, which seems to have already been tested internally by Facebook employees, would represent an alternative to collective work in the presence when there is no opportunity to carry it out.

Rethink remote working with horizon workrooms from Facebook

Since the beginning of the pandemic, giants like Google and Microsoft have worked hard to create solutions designed to optimize remote work, which has increased dramatically and suddenly, finding many companies not ready to deal with remote business management. Platforms like Microsoft Viva, for example, have been designed to make this task easier by facilitating collaboration between colleagues and remote task management. With Horizon Workrooms Facebook wants to take another step, rethinking the concept of remote work and trying to "recreate" the feeling of " presence", regardless of the physical distance between people.

The platform was designed to make remote communication more efficient compared to traditional meetings carried out by videoconference, in which it is often not possible to grasp elements of non-verbal communication that generally make conversations more fluid and pleasant.

The newly launched beta version can be downloaded for free on Oculus Quest 2, a virtual reality headset created by Oculus (owned by Facebook) available for the moment only in some countries.

How do Workrooms work?

Together with the press release, Facebook has published a video in which it is possible to preview the interface of the platform in this video it is possible to see users and their avatars performing some work tasks remotely, using their Workrooms.

Specifically, it is a virtual meeting room that can be accessed from anywhere in the world. You can access it with your customizable avatar, using the virtual reality viewer, or simply with a computer. Each meeting allows sixteen people to participate in virtual reality, while up to fifty can join in a video call.

To make the experience more immersive, the Workrooms platform allows users to use their hands instead of controllers (generally used in virtual reality environments) to perform movements with their avatar, however, it is necessary to activate the function "Hand tracking" featured on Oculus Quest and Quest 2.

For now, Facebook seems to have embraced this vision more than any other tech company, focusing in particular on developing a system that will allow people to experience virtual reality and augmented reality using fairly realistic avatars capable of increasing and improving the perception of being. physically in the same room, even if you are in different countries. As Zuckerberg said in the post, "Horizon Workrooms is another step into the metaverse."

Owning Whatsapp, Instagram and the virtual reality viewer company Oculus gives Facebook a great advantage in this sense: the company already has privileged access to a large amount of data relating to online behaviors, interests, preferences, and personalities of the users, which allows you to take advantage of the information available for the development of a pleasant and immersive virtual environment.

Mark Zuckerberg in the published post refers to a possible future application of the metaverse, presenting Workrooms in this way: "in the future, working together will be for people one of the main ways of using the metaverse".

CHAPTER 20: BLOCKTOPIA

Until a couple of years ago it was enough for a company to claim to be blockchain-based to be considered innovative and future-oriented. Today, the industry is full of platforms claiming to be scalable, fast, secure, and developer-friendly, so companies need to find other ways to win against the competition.

Interdisciplinary partnerships can make a difference and bring something innovative on board. For example, when blockchain projects have encountered the IoT in the recent past, they have always been greeted with interest by investors, entrepreneurs, and users.

Accelerated by the COVID-19 crisis that required a new communication model, the metaverse is the new virtual world in which people can share fascinating experiences with other humans even when they can't be together. The metaverse will allow people to do things together that they would not be able to do in the physical world, and scary as it may sound, it is the inevitable future reality.

International research firm Strategy Analytics has predicted that the global Metaverse market could reach a whopping $ 280 billion valuation by 2025.

Often expressed in spectacularly lit high-tech urban environments, the metaverse combines augmented reality and virtual reality. Social connection, entertainment, games, fitness, work, education, and commerce combine to create a materialized Internet where people interact and are a vital part of the experience, not just passively watching it. Let's explore what it means to collaborate with Bloktopia and what this futuristic project is.

What is Bloktopia?

Bloktopia is a 21 million story VR skyscraper, honoring 21 million Bitcoin. It is the VR metaverse that aims to become the hub of edutainment entertainment for all levels of crypto experience.

The high-tech tower emerges from a decaying world and is based on an NFT-based economy that allows entrepreneurs to own land and develop it as virtual real estate, with advertisements and events creating opportunities for revenue for users.

Cryptocurrencies, blockchain technology, VR, and AR come together to create a decentralized hub for future entrepreneurs, investors, gamers, and developers.

Supported by the Polygon network and built on a cross-platform game engine, Unity, by the founders of Sony Playstation VR, Bloktopia allows visitors to engage in basic or advanced learning, earn income, play with friends, create networks, and much more.

Bloktopia is like a mall, where stores sit alongside other types of businesses and businesses, where crypto projects, exchanges, influencers, or brands show off their content and key messages.

Bloktopians are BLOK token holders and members of the Bloktopia metaverse. For the first time, users will have access to cryptographic information and engaging content in one place.

Bloktopians will be able to learn, play, and earn money through real estate, ad revenue, and more. Based on the 3D Creation Engine, the world's most advanced real-time video game engine, Bloktopia will leverage technology to create stunning visualizations and user experiences.

The Bloktopia metaverse will consist of real estate blocks that can be purchased and governed by BLOK token holders.

Learn, earn, play and create (The four pillars of the Bloktopia metaverse)

Learn

Bloktopia will be the central hub where users can learn about the world of cryptocurrencies, which can be difficult to explore.

To gain

Bloktopians will have many income opportunities by buying real estate and even speculating on it, reselling for profit, or renting to a tenant. Other opportunities will include passive earning, staking, and advertising.

Play

Users can relax, have fun, socialize and compete with friends through first-person interaction in the world of virtual reality.

Create

Through a simple creation tool, users will be able to use their creativity by producing scenes, and works of art and even participating in events to win prizes.

The tokenized decentralized VR encrypted skyscraper

Blok tokens allow its holders to purchase NFTs, which represent the ownership of REBLOK and ADBLOK. Buying real estate within Bloktopia is known as REBLOK, which can be either sole proprietorship, represented by a single NFT, or jointly owned and represented by multiple NFTs.

REBLOK can also be rented for an event or long-term to tenants, just like real-world properties. The main locations include levels 1, 6, and 21. The Land Sale portal will be available soon and, in the meantime, CoinMarketCap has also recently secured a shop in a prime location of the Bloktopia skyscraper.

ADBLOK is the revenue stream generated by Bloktopia's advertisements. Creating hype and fame for Bloktopia brand partners through dwell time and playback speed provides a valuable perspective to advertisers. A portion of these generated advertising fees will be redistributed to Bloktopia token holders.

Who will visit Bloktopia?

According to a recent study, 90% of Bloktopia visitors will be males between 18 and 34 years old. They have a keen interest in cryptocurrencies and NFTs and make between $ 20K and $ 50K. They heard about cryptocurrencies in the news and focused on the markets of the US, Asia, and the UK.

CHAPTER 21: YIELD GUILD GAMES

Yield Guild Games (YGG) is a gaming association focused on play-to-earn blockchain games. It is a community that invests in NFTs and connects blockchain players from all over the world. Their goal is to build a network of players and investors to help each other grow together in the NFT gaming ecosystem.

Since the success of Axie Infinity, the ecosystem of play-to-earn (P2E) blockchain games has grown rapidly. Even though the P2E trend has attracted millions of people around the world, NFT gaming is not affordable for many players, especially in developing countries. Yield Guild Games is building a P2E community and offering a solution for these players so they can start playing an NFT game.

Yield Guild Games (YGG) is a decentralized autonomous organization (DAO) that invests in non-fungible tokens (NFTs) used in blockchain games. These games are part of a larger concept known as a metaverse

The idea of creating a global play-to-earn gaming community was born in 2018. Gabby Dizon, co-founder, and CEO of YGG noted that blockchain gaming was trending in Southeast Asia. At the time, many players were looking to start playing Axie Infinity, but they didn't have the money to buy the in-game NFT characters called Axie.

Realizing that blockchain gaming could be an inspiring tool for those living in developing countries, Dizon began lending its Axies to other players who couldn't afford to buy their own. This inspired him to cofound Yield Guild Games with Beryl Li in 2020 to help players grow in the world of NFT and blockchain gaming.

How does Yield Guild Games work?

Yield Guild Games combines decentralized finance (DeFi) and NFTs to create a metaverse economy on the Ethereum blockchain. The YGG DAO is an open-source protocol with rules applied through smart contracts. It serves many different purposes, such as executing community-voted governance decisions, issuing rewards, and facilitating NFT rentals.

YGG is made up of multiple SubDAOs, made up of groups of players from a specific NFT game or geographic location. Each SubDAO has its own rules for managing the business and assets of their respective play-to-earn games.

This model allows players of the same NFT game to work together to maximize profits within the game. It also allows group members to rent and use community-owned NFTs to earn in-game rewards. In return, those who lend their NFTs through the DAO can share a portion of the player's earnings. On YGG, all NFTs and digital assets are held within the community-controlled YGG Treasury. The treasure provides the NFTs to each SubDAO and includes the P2E assets of multiple blockchain games.

YGG Scholarship

To maximize the value and usefulness of NFT gaming, YGG DAO uses an NFT rental program, known as a scholarship. The idea was initially pioneered by the Axie Infinity community to offer benefits to both NFT owners and play-to-earn players.

In Axie Infinity, Axie owners can lend their gaming assets to help new players get started, in exchange for a percentage of their in-game rewards. The process is done via a smart contract on the blockchain so that students can only use these NFTs in the game. Only the manager (owner) can trade or transfer NFTs.

Similarly, YGG offers scholarships to new players as part of a revenue-sharing model, where they can get NFT assets to start playing and earn in-game rewards. Students do not need to invest money upfront but share a portion of their earnings with their managers. In addition to NFTs, new players will also receive training and guidance from community managers. YGG Scholarships are not limited to Axie Infinity NFTs. YGG Treasury, among other play-to-earn games, also owns virtual lands in The Sandbox and League of Kingdoms, virtual cars in F1 Delta Time.

SubDAO

As mentioned, YGG's DAO is mainly composed of SubDAOs. You can think of SubDAOs as communities located within the main YGG DAO. These local communities are made up of players from a specific location or P2E game. For example, there is a SubDAO dedicated to Axie Infinity players, a

SubDAO for The Sandbox players, another SubDAO for Southeast Asian players, and so on. By grouping players into different SubDAOs, they can discuss game strategies and help each other to maximize performance.

Each SubDAO manages its respective gaming activities and assets according to its own rules and conditions but still contributes to the profits of YGG DAO. In a SubDAO, there is a community lead, a wallet, and a SubDAO token. Token holders can share the returns generated by the game, based on their contributions. In addition, they can make suggestions and vote on governance decisions related to the SubDAO, such as whether to buy multiple NFTs in-game or how to manage their assets.

What is the YGG token?

Yield Guild Games (YGG) is an ERC-20 token that grants holders the right to participate in the governance of the YGG DAO. It has a total offering of 1 billion tokens and 25 million YGG was sold via an Initial DEX Offering (IDO) on SushiSwap in 2021. To support the community, YGG set aside 45% of the total offering to be phased out to users, over four years.

As the platform's native token, YGG is used to pay for services on the network. It can also be staked to earn rewards in YGG Vaults or used to unlock exclusive content on YGG's Discord channel. Additionally, YGG holders can submit proposals and vote on decisions related to the group's technology, products, projects, token distribution, and global governance structure. Winning tips that are ultimately implemented on the DAO will be rewarded with YGG tokens.

YGG Vault

YGG DAO takes a different yield farming approach than most DeFi staking platforms. Typically, tokens are staked to earn a fixed rate of interest. On YGG, each vault represents a token reward program for a specific activity that YGG manages. For example, one vault may provide performance-based returns from a scholarship program, while another rewards stakers based on the breeding program on Axie.

YGG also plans to develop an all-in-one super index vault that represents all the return-generating assets in its ecosystem. This vault will reward stakers based on group revenue from subscriptions, merchandise, rentals, treasury growth, and performance of the SubDAO index.

Token holders can stake in relation to the business they support and the rewards will be distributed in proportion to the amount of YGG they stake via smart contracts. Depending on how the vault is programmed, the rewards may also include YGG, Ether (ETH), or stable coin tokens.

How to buy YGG on Binance?

You can buy Yield Guild Games (YGG) on exchanges such as Binance.

1. Log into your Binance account and click on [Trading]. Choose [Classic] or [Advanced] trading mode to get started.
2. Click on [BTC / USDT] to open the search bar and type "YGG" to see the available trading pairs. We will use YGG / BUSD as an example.

3. Go to the [Spot] box on the right and enter the amount of YGG to buy. In this example, we will use a market order. Click on [Buy YGG] to confirm the order and the purchased YGGs will be credited to your Spot Wallet.

Closing

Through a unique revenue-sharing model, YGG is building a decentralized community in the real world. It offers participants the opportunity to grow in these virtual worlds through an innovative gaming economy. As metaverse projects grow, NFT groups such as Yield Guild Games could benefit from the influence of newcomers and crypto enthusiasts who wish to explore NFT games to earn an alternative source of income.

CHAPTER 22: WHAT IS ENJIN?

———— ❋ ————

Enjin is the cryptocurrency linked to the world of online games. Gamers, it is known, are particularly attentive to the regularity of online gaming, and in this regard, ENJ Coin aims to create a gaming community characterized by transparency and safety. All these tools allow you to develop dedicated websites, gaming forums, and marketplaces where you can buy and sell game items (NFT) and earn money from their gaming experience.

The story of Enjin

The need to optimize online gaming platforms was spotted in 2017 by blockchain-savvy programmer Maxime Blagov, also an established gamer. With his colleague Witek Radomski he thought and planned the establishment of the Enjin project. After months of planning and testing, he went online with his token in August of the same year.

The ICO, which ended less than a month later, ceased following a pre-sale gain of $12 million, and a total of $23 million. The improvements gradually improved over the following months, and in the first quarter of 2018 Enjin was already available for Android and iOS, in the middle of the year, Enjin released the first plugins. One of them, for example, was the one applied to the famous video game Minecraft.

Another is the game engine called Unity SDK, in turn, is considered by numerous video game developers, who have therefore brought Enjin technology under the eyes of 770 million users around the world.

The Enjin roadmap was and is quite evident: the more developers adopt the features of the Enjin coin, the more players use the Enjin coin, which by exporting its potential is destined to spread more and more and grow in value.

How does Enjin work?

Enjin, as we have said, aims to create a real ecosystem for gamers and video game developers, to guarantee safety, innovations, and fun. Enjin has brought particular features that are generating great changes within the world of online video games.

First of all, the so-called Enjin Website Builder: a function that allows you to help users (whether players or developers) to generate web portals quickly and free of charge within the platform. Many will know how useful it can be, once they become passionate about a video game, a reference website for fans where they can compare, suggest and help.

Enj coin: the native coin of the Enjin project was created to help users manage and exchange (by buying or selling) game-related goods, (such as weapons, clothes, money, and much more, depending of course on the game in question).

All virtual goods that are bought or sold are assigned to an account, in turn, managed by a platform whose consultation is extremely simple. Due to Smart Contracts, all transaction details are recorded in the blockchain, suggesting a certain regularity and transparency, so no one will be able to cheat and the games will keep integrity.

Mobile apps: Enjin works on both Android and iOS so that practically every user can play or consult the dedicated forums even from their smartphone.

ENJ Mining (How are Enjin Coins created?)

Enjin tokens are of the ERC20 type, developed on the Ethereum platform. The Enjin platform is moving forward with the implementation of a channel-based solution similar to the Lightning Network, which would allow the network to improve its scalability potential.

The minting process of personalized coins will be performed through the so-called "Mint" function of the smart contract, which will be made accessible through web, mobile, and API-based user interfaces.

Enjin also has full support for ERC-1155 resources. Its blockchain explorer EnjinX was the first to provide users with access to such resources.

Users can now explore the world of ERC-1155 blockchain assets and collectibles, search for assets and collections by name, address, and token ID, and verify ownership, rarity, provenance, and authenticity of tokens.

This is a universal catalog of all in-game objects (NFTs) from the entire Enjin multiverse. This means that players can now easily browse game items and see when they were created, who created them, who owns them, what they do, and how to acquire them. The immutable transparency of the blockchain was thus also transposed to the world of games.

Coin Distribution ENJ (How many Enjins are available?)

As of March 2021, Enjin covers a market cap of $ 2.2 billion, with a token supply of $ 934 million. The supply will reach its maximum limit when 1 billion coins are paid out. At that point, the algorithm will cease to ensure that new Enjin Coins are produced and the gamer market will only have to use the coins produced up to then.

In the same period, the single Enjin Coin token has a value that is around 2.4 dollars.

Also for Enjin, the period between the end of 2020 and the beginning of 2021 was of great satisfaction: closing 2020 at $ 0.14, dragged by the upward race of Bitcoin at the beginning of 2021, it recorded an increase of 1405. % in just three months.

What are the uses of the Enjin platform?

The Enjin platform allows you to create and manage blockchain games, without the complexity of building and maintaining any blockchain infrastructure or writing any code related to it. It is a robust, flexible, and powerful tool of services for creating innovative blockchain games. Overall it is made up of four separate but interconnected parts.

Trusted Cloud is the main backend service of the Enjin platform; is a cloud-hosted service that connects games to the Ethereum blockchain. The platform API allows developers to query and send commands to the Enjin platform. Wallet Deamon is a tool used to automate the authorization of transaction requests to and from the Trusted Cloud. Blockchain SDK is an SDK for Unity. Some SDKs have been released for Java, Godot, and GraphQL.

Enjin's Smart Wallet: is it safe?

It is possible to take advantage of a Smart Wallet that supports Bitcoin, Ethereum, Litecoin, Enjin Coin, and all the other coins that use the ERC-20 protocol. Enjin also supports virtual items from every reputable platform you add and effortlessly syncs with your Ethereum address. This includes the ERC-721 and ERC-1155 tokens.

You will be able to exchange coins and virtual game items with any other Smart Wallet user within the wallet. There is support for transaction requests which can be sent to other wallet owners, who will then either confirm or deny the transaction. Additionally, rules or thresholds can be set to prevent unauthorized or unwanted transactions from occurring.

Enjin Smart Wallet was created with security in mind and one of the best security features is the secure keyboard developed for Enjin Smart Wallet. This keyboard is natively part of the app and prevents keyloggers or snoopers from seeing or capturing anything you type, including passwords and private keys. And for those who are particularly security conscious, the wallet can also be configured to randomize your keys.

The further addition to the security of the wallet consists of two separate layers of encryption. The hardware layer includes Advanced Encryption Standard, and the software uses custom software encryption to encrypt all data processed by the wallet. The wallet will also block any registration or screenshot of the wallet itself at the operating system level. If you are not interested in all these features and security, you can also keep your Enjin coins in any ERC-20 compatible wallet, such as MetaMask, Ledger, or Trezor.

Concluding opinions on the ENJ coin

By placing gaming assets on the blockchain, Enjin aims to prevent fraud and counterfeiting. It would be a huge improvement for the gaming industry and gamers, and with the huge customer base that Enjin already has, the coin should be able to achieve quite significant large-scale adoption.

Having said that, Enjin undoubtedly remains a new project and is still to be tested in all its features. The partnership that the platform has in place with Unity should help guide them towards the important goal of creating real games on the blockchain, and this will help channel further adoption of the Enjin Coin. Nothing has been proven yet, but the project looks to have a promising future.

Even the same addition we mentioned related to the blockchain explorer which turns out to be rather easy to use, a dedicated Smart Wallet, and a real internal market that allows players to easily buy and sell the resources acquired in the Enjin multiverse, are all pieces of a well thought out puzzle.

The continued expansion will likely promote ever new adoption, but what the project needs now is a successful game, attracting millions of players from around the world. With such a forerunner, Enjin could take both the ENJ coin and the related game multiverse to hitherto unthinkable levels.

CHAPTER 23: STAR ATLAS

———— ❈ ————

Those who love space-themed video games, on the other hand, will be happy to know that in the Metaverse there is Star Atlas, a multiplayer set in 2.620. Excellent graphics, which are based on the Nanite technology of Unreal Engine 5 offers an engaging and quality experience, equal to that of cinema, while the cryptocurrency system is managed by the Solana blockchain. It has over 200 operational nodes around the world and can manage over 50,000 transactions per second.

The gameplay of Star Atlas involves managing the ongoing conflict between three factions vying for political domination. It is about acting wisely to earn resources and rewards and win over other competitors. Furthermore, while engaging in these virtual battles, cities and microeconomics can be created to lead some decentralized autonomous organizations (DAOs) that allow you to take control of certain territories.

In Star Atlas, there are two cryptocurrencies, Atlas and Polis that can be used to trade, obtain and create non-fungible tokens (NFT). Assets and properties can be spent and exchanged for-profit and liquidity. The peculiarity of Star Atlas is decentralization: in fact, the tokens can be used in the secondary markets of NFT.

The average value of Atlas and Polis is around 4.70 euros. Star Atlas is a play-to-earn, open world, strategic MMORPG set in space, whose game mechanics, and therefore the related NFT are completely in the hands of the users. All good intentions were enough to make the hype skyrocket and create a community that registers 160,000 users on Discord. It wants to be, in effect, a triple-A title built on Solana, which aims to exploit the speed of a blockchain capable of guaranteeing, thanks to its protocol, over 50 thousand transactions per second.

Before going into detail and understanding Solana's fundamental role in the video game, a general look at the project is useful. The role of the blockchain on which the game is built is to guarantee a massive amount of in-game transactions, dictated by exploration, resource extraction, trade exchanges, Seen from an even broader perspective, Star Atlas aims to recreate a world with its economy and politics, on which depend strategies, trade routes, productive lands, and everything that could come from them. A metaverse in its most utopian concept in which a player can find the opportunity to combine their video game passion with the improvement of their in-game activities, monetizing them.

All in an immersive 3D interface, with cinematic-quality graphics obtained thanks to Unreal Engine. The gameplay is inevitably intertwined with in-game economic aspects (even if this definition is reductive, given the nature of a play-to-earn). Players will have to deal with a galactic-sized map, where they can track down resources as they explore. They will be able to refine them, exploit them or trade them, but all assuming the risk of losing their rewards during the research. This depends in the first place on the structure of the game, at the foundation of which there is an essential tripartition.

All new players (you can do this right away by joining their Solana wallet) must first choose one of the three-game factions. There is the MUD Group, which is made up of people specializing in firefighting and technology, the Ustur, the professional cybernetic researchers, and, finally, the ONI Group, a kind of alliance of different types of aliens. For all of them, the playroom is divided into so many security levels.

The second fundamental variable is represented by ships or vehicles for exploration. Each accessible area is an asset in itself and more remote areas can be difficult to reach, so sufficient resources are needed to enable research. Players can also control their ships manually to discover the riches of the game universe through special scanning modules.

Adjacent to, but in symbiosis with, ships are stations that include warehousing and trading functions, shipyards and repairs, materials refineries, retail centers, crew recruitment, training areas, and more. If that sounds like a lot, we're just getting started. The whole economy of the game is based on these stations, which make it easier to explore the playing field through the installation of "jumping points" or wormholes.

Building on such a large and complex system, Star Atlas also encourages the creation of internal teams or guilds, to create joint competitions between players, but to use features that can be used through mass participation. For example, the creation of a DAC (Decentralized Automated Authorization System), a type of space city with its internal economy controlled by several members of the same group.

Atlas and Polis

The value of anything Star Atlas can only revolve around its reward system, as part of a balanced economy also guaranteed by game mechanics. As mentioned, there are two cryptocurrencies, namely ATLAS and POLISH.

ATLAS is the in-game currency. Basically, it will be used for any type of operation within Star Atlas, starting with the acquisition of ships, resources, crews, territories, etc. And all these dynamics are included in the reflection of a real economy that the game wants to revive, such as trade, whether with NPCs or between peers, or operating expenses, such as payments for fuel, repairs, or Staff. It already plays a predominant role in the market.

POLIS, on the other hand, is the dominance token. For what is the vision of Star Atlas, players will have to manage not only their resources but also those of entire territories. In such a context, necessarily shared with other players, a structure of a political nature will be needed to support not only the interests of individuals but of the entire gaming universe. The political influence of a player (or group of players) is represented by the POLIS token, which will determine the jurisdictional conditions of the territories, based on the use that the players will make of it.

If it may seem complicated, an example might be simply managing a territory by imposing taxes on other players or drafting a series of laws to be enforced and decided by a group. And all this regardless of the owner of the territory in question. In the DAC (Decentralized Autonomous Corporation), which we have already mentioned, POLIS allows players to express their voting rights by pushing them to cooperate in other to prevent other larger and coordinated groups, possibly, from taking over their territory.

This dynamic is reminiscent of the functional development of DAO (Decentralized Autonomous Organization), and the only difference is the different fields of activity. If the DAC has an operation in the in-game world, the DAO has it in the real world. And in fact, the functions of POLIS are not limited to the game universe, on the contrary, the governance token will allow the Star Atlas community to influence the decision-making process of the development team. But this will still take some time. "A political structure will be needed, to govern not only the interests of individuals but of the entire game universe."

The ships

As mentioned, ships (or ships, in short) are a fundamental element in the game. Therefore, if you want to buy one, the choice must be well considered, especially before such a large variety of the offer. The development team has already anticipated the existence of 120 ship models (not all yet available), which are divided into categories and subcategories.

The first distinction consists of 9 different manufacturers, the identity of the manufacturer will have different consequences in the exploration of the different territories. Each ship varies in size, function (transport, combat, exploration, etc.), and rarity.

Finally, different modules can be applied to each ship, interchangeable and optimized, with different in-game features. The size, more specifically, also depends on the number of slots available to the crew and based on that the license required to use the ship in the game varies (yes, a license is required to steer the ship). To date, there are 27 ships available on the market, but they will continue to be listed over the months, also because the development of the game depends on their sale, helping them to keep the team's finances stable.

Score (minigame)

This is certainly very pleasant. But to pilot your ship in the Star Atlas universe, we will have to wait a long time. Meanwhile, players can try their hand at the Star Atlas "mini-game", a browser-based game in which ships purchased from the market can generate significant revenue.

The mini-game consists in dedicating its assets (ships) to its faction, in conflict (according to the lore) with the others. To participate in the battle, the mini-game asks you to dedicate the necessary resources to your fleet, namely food, fuel, repair kits, and ammunition, all available on the market, to be recharged, from time to time once exhausted. From a certain point of view, it is nothing more than a form of staking your assets, however, the rewards can only be obtained if you maintain a sufficient level of resources to devote to ships.

The ROI (rate of return on investment) is estimated at 100% per year, with a monthly APR of between 7% and 15%. Which, of course, is subject to the value of ATLAS over time. Like all play-to-earn video games, the goal of Star Atlas is to revolutionize the world of video game entertainment, which is necessarily linked to that of finance, but also a new notion of "business", more in the real world but a metaverse, perhaps combining pleasure and profit. And of all the existing projects, that of Star Atlas is certainly among the most promising.

CHAPTER 24 FORTNITE

———◆———

The Metaverse is the last frontier of the web and beyond, a revolution that is destined to be talked about and to make enormous changes in everyone's life. Just recently, Epic Games, the company that created Fortnite, declared its desire to create a metaverse, and it is immediately moving in this direction. Fortnite is enriching itself with Fortnite Party Worlds, virtual universes where you don't fight, but you can participate with friends and have fun in different situations.

The Metaverse is an opportunity that appeals to everyone for the enormous potential that this world that combines virtual and augmented reality seems to offer in the coming years. That's why the big names in the gaming sector didn't miss this opportunity and some have already started to take their first steps.

Fortnite, for example, is already a game that is well suited to the dynamics of the metaverse that sees the possibility of interacting in a virtual world through 3D avatars to be customized with skins and accessories. Not just games, but also events, parties, and other opportunities to get to know each other and socialize. It is not the first time that live concerts and even premieres of movie trailers have been organized in the Fortnite world, situations that, until recently, were unimaginable. A prime example of this type of event was Travis Scott's virtual concert, which took place in April 2020, and was attended by over 12.3 million simultaneous players, many more than the previous record of 10.7 million attendees. during the Marshmello concert in 2019.

Fortnite, according to Lego Ventures, has embarked on its journey to becoming the "first reliable meta version" of the video game industry. The house that made Fortnite, Epic Games, has received a lot of funding. It all seems to amount to about a billion dollars, and supporters include Sony and other large companies waiting to enter the metaverse.

New game modes for Fortnite

Fortnite is becoming a real prototype of the Metaverse and many new maps are already available for exciting game modes. At the moment, it is Walnut World (Noceto Faceto) created by five walnuts (code 9705-9549-4193), a virtual environment that reproduces an amusement park, and Late Night Lounge (Salotto Nottambulo) created by TreyJTH (code 8868-0043-1912) where you can socialize and interact with other users.

This new game mode that starts Fortnite towards the Metaverse, or the Party World, are independent worlds and evolution of the game dynamics aimed more at creating entertainment and socialization. Users can access these maps through their three-dimensional characters and manage their emotions, but they cannot yet take advantage of what is a great opportunity offered by the Metaverse, namely portability, i.e. the ability to purchase virtual resources and use them elsewhere. Therefore, if Fornite cannot be defined as a metaverse, it is true that it has taken the first step in this direction by contributing to the development of this innovative technology.

CHAPTER 25: HOW TO CREATE AND SELL AN NFT

———— ❋ ————

An NFT (non-fungible token) is the registration of a digital object's certificate of ownership: NFT can be videos, texts, gifs, books, or music. Undoubtedly, NFTs are revolutionizing the art world. This historic moment must also be borne in mind. And it goes hand in hand with other of the same historic internet moments as when we downloaded the first song from Napster or registered on Myspace or found our first-class friend on Facebook or listened to ours. the first ASMR.

NFTs allow you to certify GIF, video, jpeg, mp3, text, and 3d rendering and almost all other file formats existing in the world and considered as unique works. This technology allows you to create a new type of "ownership" for digital files that were not possible before. NFTs can be bought, collected, sold, and even destroyed just like physical items. Blockchain comes with a transparent transaction and a price history that is visible to anyone with an internet connection.

What content can be considered NFT?

Potentially everything digital. Although right now it looks like the digital art world is experiencing a crazy boom! We live in a historical moment in which there is a lot of freedom of action in this regard and everything that is art, songs, recipes, manuals, books, or ideas for startups is potentially associated with the world of NFT.

NFTs have effectively become the best tool for transferring digital works from one person to another, without having to surrender copyrights with old copyrighted methods. Whether it's a meme, a Twitter message, a particular image, or even a game, anything in digital form can be sold through NFT, which certifies the possession of that idea or that digital content unequivocally.

With NFT (an acronym that means Non-Fungible Token) we identify a digital certificate that certifies the originality and possession of particular digital content. An NFT is in effect the digital correspondent of the certificate of ownership of an asset, where the "notary" is a database redistributed via blockchain, therefore impossible to falsify or modify.

Anyone who creates and sells an NFT must have the exclusivity of the idea or content: to certify this exclusive idea and therefore be the only owner, they must certify it on a blockchain, to be able to earn something from its subsequent sale (to anyone want to buy it).

With an NFT we can certify the possession of everything we create digitally: we go from a simple photo taken through the creations made by computer or other IT means, without forgetting the messages or other works created by the human intellect (for example a song written on a document, a poem made on TXT.

The main advantage of NFT is in its "infungible" nature: after having certified an NFT on the blockchain, no one else will be able to claim rights to that content, effectively replacing the concept of copyright (where to protect one's idea or own content it is necessary to register patents in each country where the content will be exploited).

Another obvious advantage of NFTs is the ease with which they can be sold: if someone is willing to buy possession of our idea, it is possible to transfer the NFT as is done with cryptocurrencies, using completely identical tools (since the certificate real is an Ethereum token).

The role of the blockchain

The blockchain has a very important role in the process of creating an NFT, it is thanks to the blockchain that we can certify the NFT, using the same cryptographic mechanisms seen to be able to create a new cryptocurrency. Currently, the blockchain that can be used to create NFT is Ethereum, which has the best features to be able to create NFT (cryptographic execution speed, management costs, and simplicity in exchange and sale), thanks to the ERC721 token standard (the most used for creating NFT) and the ERC1155 token standard. In addition to Ethereum, the Tezos, Polkadot, Cosmos, and Binance Smart Chain blockchains are also widely used, all of which are presented as alternatives or evolutions of Ethereum.

Creating a cryptocurrency wallet (which one to choose)

To create NFTs we will first have to create our virtual wallet (e-wallet) so that we can manage the NFTs and the earnings generated by the sale or exchange (in real money or cryptocurrencies). Before creating NFTs, it is necessary to create a free account on the appropriate sites, so that a wallet is immediately available in which to store the NFTs created.

For example, coinbase can be used as one of the best digital wallets that you can use for NFTs is a free account on this platform we will have all the tools available to manage digital cryptocurrency and keep the NFTs in our possession, using the Ethereum blockchain and ERC721 tokens. After the creation of the NFT, it will be immediately visible in the wallet, without having to use other sites.

We advise you to use it as a reference wallet on sites specialized in the creation of NFTs, to obtain lower commission costs or even free NFTs. Another very effective wallet for storing the NFTs that we have created or exchanged is Metamask. By installing this app on our phone it is possible to exchange NFTs with other people, keep the NFTs generated on one of the dedicated platforms, and view, clearly and efficiently, the earnings we have obtained from the sale of NFTs. The platform specializes in the exchange of Ethereum-based tokens, including the ERC721 token and the ERC1155 token on which the operation of NFTs is based.

Trust Wallet

One of the best platforms for storing and trading NFTs is Trust Wallet, which is owned by the Binance company. With a free account, you can immediately access your wallet and associate it with one of the platforms that create NFTs, so that you can immediately keep the NFTs created, sell those already in your possession, or exchange NFTs with other users in a completely safe way.

Math Wallet NFT

Another valid platform on which it is possible to store and exchange Ethereum tokens is Math Wallet. On this platform, it is possible to access your cryptocurrencies and NFTs stored by the app, by the browser extension, and by the web, with the possibility of keeping a physical copy of the wallet (cold wallet) on a dedicated key, to prevent any type of theft.

If we are looking for a very safe and efficient platform to store cryptocurrencies and NFTs, Math Wallet offers high standards of security, especially if we intend to keep large sums of cryptocurrencies or NFTs of a certain value (already purchased or to be created later).

Which works can be transformed into NFT

Non-Fungible Tokens can be used to certify any digital file. We can create NFTs for a painting, a particular text created by us, a text of a piece of music, a score of our invention, or a video that we shot with our smartphone or tablet.

Not all NFTs will have a high value or can be sold for a profit: not everything we create has such a value that we can recover the expense necessary to create an NFT! The secret lies precisely in knowing how to create real digital works of art, which can then be resold as unique pieces to collectors or to people interested in getting their hands on something unique.

The sale of NFTs (marketplaces)

NFT marketplaces provide the tools to create and sell NFTs, interfacing with the digital wallet we have created. On these platforms, we can create NFT, pay the commissions necessary for its creation, create the announcement of sale or auction and, if we find someone interested, sell the possession of the NFT (which will require a new step in blockchain to change the owner).

How much does it cost to create NFT

To create NFT we must take into account the costs related to the passage in the blockchain, which still requires certain computing power to be able to generate the required tokens. When we choose what to certify in NFT, the system may require commissions for the creation of the token, with prices that vary according to the value of the Ethereum and the type of content to be encrypted.

After creation, the token will be stored in our chosen wallet at no additional cost; at the time of sale or exchange, there are other commission costs, necessary to be able to "change owner" within the blockchain. These costs can be paid by both the old owner and the new owner, although they are often shared equally.

Some markets for NFT (OpenSea) do not charge anything in the initial phase of creation, leaving the transition to blockchain pending "until the sale"; in this way it is possible to immediately generate NFTs for free and pay the entire certification cycle required by the blockchain only in case of a sale, generating a single expense. Not all creators of NFT are filthy rich: the idea that we try to sell via NFT must be valid and have a certain value from a collector or artistic point of view so that we can resell it at a good price.

Let's not forget that even if there are platforms to create free NFTs, the cost of using the blockchain is the only difference in the period we pay these commissions (some sites look for them immediately, others only after the sale).

CHAPTER 26: COINBASE

---

oinbase, what is it for? Before we get there, perhaps it is best to understand what Coinbase is. Coinbase is a platform that allows the purchase and sale of cryptocurrencies. In technical terms, it is called a "cryptocurrency exchange". It is software where you can buy or sell digital currencies, such as Ethereum, Bitcoin, and many others.

Coinbase is estimated to be worth about $ 85 billion (on the New York Stock Exchange debut day). In Coinbase, the operation is therefore related to cryptographic exchange. Here we find people buying and buying. A slightly updated version is found at a money changer, such as an airport (even if they only work with cryptocurrencies). Coinbase was born in 2012 in San Francisco, founded by Brian Armstrong and Fred Ehrsam, who during the year of its foundation introduced the possibility of buying and selling bitcoin through classic bank transfers.

It was a huge success from the start and in just a few years, it has reached one million subscribers. Among the major milestones of the exchange are the acquisition of blockchain explorer Blocker and the company Kippt, which handled online bookmarks.

Finally, Coinbase has been the protagonist of some of the most important partnerships of recent years, with Time Inc, Expedia, Dell, and so on. The purpose of these partnerships is? Be able to accept payments in Bitcoin. Now the company is listed on the US stock exchange and the portal allows you to work on digital assets with fiat currencies in 31 countries around the world.

How Coinbase works is pretty simple starting from the registration phase. The platform plays the role of "Exchange" of cryptocurrencies, in fact, here you can buy, use or sell digital currencies. To access all the services, registration is required, which is free and streamlined in the procedure. To open the account just fill in the required fields with your data, choose a password and confirm the email that arrives, up to here everything is easy.

Once you have followed the instructions, there will be a box to fill in which will ask for the telephone number and you will then need to enter a code that will be sent to us via text message. Done, from here on you will work directly from the account page. And it will be this account, a wallet, in which the cryptocurrency will be kept. The last step is always a bit boring but necessary, insert your identity card or passport to be able to verify your identity officially.

How do you top up the wallet?

To top up your Coinbase account you can decide between two different ways:

Deposit by debit/credit card, in which case the deposit will be immediately available on your Coinbase account. Cards belonging to the VISA and Mastercard circuit are supported;

Deposit by SEPA transfer, in this case, you will have to make a transfer from your internet banking to the bank account details of the exchange and the money will take an average of 1/2 day to be credited.

Buying cryptocurrencies with Coinbase

Buying crypto with Coinbase is simple, just access the "Buy" page, choose the cryptocurrency you intend to buy, then indicate the specific amount in cryptocurrency or the local currency of reference: you will immediately see the commission that Coinbase will keep and then the actual sum that will be deposited in the chosen wallet. Once you have selected your preferred payment method, you can proceed with the purchase.

If you already have a cryptocurrency, Coinbase also allows you to convert it simply by selecting the one you want to sell and the one you want to buy.

Selling cryptocurrencies with Coinbase

To sell cryptocurrencies with Coinbase, you need to select the currency you want to sell and indicate the amount. Then you need to confirm your choice and then validate the transaction with a code received via SMS. Fees also apply here.

Withdraw money from the account

It is also possible to withdraw, but you must first check your bank account. To withdraw, simply select the item "Withdrawal" and from which account to make it (it will take the usual SEPA transfer times).

CHAPTER 27: EARTH 2

---

orn last November, Earth 2 is attracting many users thanks to the possible earning opportunities. Let's find out what it is and how the service works. What is Earth 2? How does it work? You have probably heard of earth2.io on social networks given the high interest in this project registered in recent times. This mysterious service, born last November, is becoming more and more popular and is conquering many users, mostly attracted by possible revenue opportunities. So let's find out together what it is and how it works.

Earth 2 (what it is and how it works)

So let's start with the main question, what is Earth 2? The site describes it as "the beginning of the future virtual existence of our world" and claims that we have the "chance to own part of this incredible future".

In what is currently referred to as "Phase 1", Earth 2 is a service that replicates the world at a 1: 1 scale in a digital representation and divides it into tiles of approximately 10 square meters. Each of these tiles, which corresponds to the same area present in reality, can be purchased for a certain amount. The value of these land slots can depend on several factors and can be resold to other service users.

Earth 2 recreates the Earth in detail, with constructions, buildings, land, and vegetation, through more than 5 trillion unique tiles: these are visible via a web map very similar to Google Maps, and Mapbox, where you can find all of them. Features, including size, value, owner, and other details. That's all Earth 2 is today simply, a shared map with a grid, with land to buy and resell.

For the future, however, the developers promise great things and Earth 2 should become a real game and virtual world. At the moment, however, there are no further details, everything remains shrouded in mystery. On the earth2.io site, it can be read that the world of Earth 2 will progressively see other Phases with different levels of play and users will also have the possibility to build buildings in the places they own.

Earth 2 (how do you make money with the virtual world?)

Earth 2 is built to generate income for those who own the territories. At the moment there are three methods to have some economic return:

- Sale: the price of the individual cards starts from very low figures (even from 0.10 dollars) and is destined to fluctuate over time with the evolution of the market,
- Income tax ("Land income tax"): is calculated per property based on the class of land per country and the sales of cards in the same country,
- Code: each user has a code that can be sent to friends or other users for the purchase of tiles with 5% credit in exchange.

Earth 2 (methods of payment and withdrawal of money)

To buy free passes, the "Buy Land" section is available, while the "Marketplace" section is a sort of secondary market, where you can buy a land already owned by others and offered for sale.

The purchase of land can be done through PayPal, or through the credits in the account balance, added previously. Withdrawing the money in the account for moving to your current account at the moment occurs in a fairly complex way, although the developers of the project have already ensured that there will be significant improvements in the future.

For information, simply access the "Settings, Withdraw Funds" section: you must manually send an e-mail message from the same address used for the Earth 2 account with various information (full name, address, account name, e-mail address) email, a name that appears on the bank account, account number, telephone number and the amount you intend to withdraw).

Earth 2 (virtual world and real risks)

Is Earth 2 reliable? Is the money "invested" in the virtual world safe or are we facing yet another scam? In the section "Our team" you can find some information on the founder, the Australian Shane Isaac, and on the other members of the Earth 2 team around the world.

Some are also quite well-known names in the tech world, such as Oculus VR co-founder. There are also links to the various LinkedIn profiles, where you can browse to find out more about the team members. Oculus VR co-founder Dillon Seo follows Earth 2 from his private Facebook account and confirms his partnership on LinkedIn himself. Mapbox CEO Eric Gunderson follows Earth 2 on Twitter with a verified account.

At the moment on Earth 2, there are very few certainties about the reliability and net of an updated contact page, it seems the staff is still too poorly structured, and also the company data of the company behind the project are missing. For now, maximum caution, it is important not to be enticed immediately by going to spend thousands of euros in search of easy earnings, because the risk of not revising your money exists.

www.ingramcontent.com/pod-product-compliance
Lightning Source LLC
Chambersburg PA
CBHW071423210326
41597CB00020B/3635